SUPER-STICKY WECHAT AND CHINESE SOCIETY

SUPER-STICKY WECHAT AND CHINESE SOCIETY

BY

YUJIE CHEN
University of Leicester, UK

ZHIFEI MAO
The Chinese University of Hong Kong, China

JACK LINCHUAN QIU
The Chinese University of Hong Kong, China

United Kingdom – North America – Japan
India – Malaysia – China

Emerald Publishing Limited
Howard House, Wagon Lane, Bingley BD16 1WA, UK

First edition 2018

Copyright © 2018 Emerald Publishing Limited

Reprints and permissions service
Contact: permissions@emeraldinsight.com

No part of this book may be reproduced, stored in a retrieval system, transmitted in any form or by any means electronic, mechanical, photocopying, recording or otherwise without either the prior written permission of the publisher or a license permitting restricted copying issued in the UK by The Copyright Licensing Agency and in the USA by The Copyright Clearance Center. Any opinions expressed in the chapters are those of the authors. Whilst Emerald makes every effort to ensure the quality and accuracy of its content, Emerald makes no representation implied or otherwise, as to the chapters' suitability and application and disclaims any warranties, express or implied, to their use.

British Library Cataloguing in Publication Data
A catalogue record for this book is available from the British Library

ISBN: 978-1-78743-092-1 (Print)
ISBN: 978-1-78743-091-4 (Online)
ISBN: 978-1-78743-944-3 (Epub)

Printed and bound by CPI Group (UK) Ltd, Croydon, CR0 4YY

ISOQAR certified
Management System,
awarded to Emerald
for adherence to
Environmental
standard
ISO 14001:2004.

Certificate Number 1985
ISO 14001

INVESTOR IN PEOPLE

ACKNOWLEDGEMENTS

The authors are grateful to Alex Bruns and Jennifer McCall, who showed initial interests in the project. We owe Jen for her incredible patience and support to make this book happen. The anonymous reviewers and Angela X. Wu offered valuable feedback and comments on the manuscript. We would also like to thank Ying Chen for introducing us to the WeChat Team and Jianhong Guan for sharing many WeChat's publications. Finally, special thanks go to Jen McCall (again), Rachel Ward, and everyone at Emerald Publishing for guiding this book for publication.

CONTENTS

About the Authors		ix
Introduction		1
1.	A Silver-spoon App: WeChat, Tencent and the Mobile Revolution	19
2.	Super-sticky Design and Everyday Cultures	47
3.	The Eventful WeChat	77
4.	Conclusion: Super-sticky WeChat and the Global Society	103
Appendix		115
References		121
Index		145

ABOUT THE AUTHORS

Yujie ('Julie') Chen is a Lecturer in the Department of Media, Communication, and Sociology at the University of Leicester. Her research interests focus on how technology shifts the employment structure and work culture in general. She has published works on theorizing digital labor, on-demand work and platform economy, and platform labor and algorithmic activism among taxi drivers in China. She is now working on a book that investigates into how and why data labor tends to be ignored and treated as invisible in the rise of the so-called Big Data era.

Zhifei Mao works in the School of Journalism and Communication at The Chinese University of Hong Kong. Her research interests are in risk society and China, environmental communication, new media studies, and communication of financial risk. Her forthcoming book (with Routledge) investigates how risk culture is played out in Chinese stock market whose unpredictability often baffles Western investors and scholars alike. Prior to her current position, she has worked with Professor Ulrich Beck on the project 'Methodological Cosmopolitanism—In the Laboratory of Climate Change' (funded by ERC) and with Professor Joseph Chan and Professor Jack Qiu on media events in greater China, respectively.

Jack Linchuan Qiu is a Professor in the School of Journalism and Communication at The Chinese University of Hong Kong. He is the author of *Goodbye iSlave: A Manifesto for Digital Abolition* and *Working-Class Network Society: Communication Technology and the Information Have-Less in Urban China.*

INTRODUCTION

I.1. RISE OF A MEGA-PLATFORM

Jay was born in Detroit, Michigan, but he has worked for more than 10 years as a photographer in Shanghai, China, a mega-city of 24 million. Jay describes his lifestyle as 'very Chinese.'[1] To buy his breakfast or other mundane business transactions, Jay does not usually need to carry his wallet around. Instead, he scans a QR code via WeChat Pay (a virtual wallet operating similar to Apple Pay). He talks with his coworkers and friends mainly through WeChat audio messaging because 'they would feel strange if you ring them.' Jay has taught his family members in the US how to use WeChat so that they can have video chats on a regular basis without paying exorbitant fees for international calls or SMS.

Jay probably would have never realised how entrenched WeChat has become in his everyday life until he signed up for a 12-hour WeChat Sabbath experiment initiated by WeChat. When the experiment started, the first thing Jay found himself doing was to stop by an ATM to withdraw cash. When regular work hour started, he faced an immediate challenge – he did not have the phone number of the sponsor with whom he had to work that day because they normally communicate through WeChat. Without access to WeChat, Jay ended up calling a mutual friend to ask for his sponsor's number. By the time Jay reached his sponsor, he already missed the appointment. In the evening, he missed his regular video chat with his daughter in the US because of WeChat Sabbath.

As the 12-hour fast on WeChat ended, Jay confessed, 'leaving WeChat means leaving [social] life' in Shanghai. Jay takes for granted many of the services that he can get by tapping into his WeChat account without noticing how his daily routine and social life have come to rely on WeChat. WeChat is now inseparable from its users' everyday habits: checking status updates from their friends, purchasing items from local stores or online shops, hailing a taxi and transferring money (Hariharan, 2017). One tends to underestimate the power of habits until the routine is disrupted. As bestseller author Charles Duhigg pointed out, '[habits] often occur without our permission […] They shape our lives far more than we realize […]' (2012, p. 25).

'Leaving WeChat means leaving [social] life' in China – think about it for a moment. To some who have never used WeChat, this statement may sound hyperbolic. But to many Chinese and people like Jay who live in Chinese cities, this is not at all an exaggeration. As researchers who use and are familiar with WeChat, we also see something extra about this app – or, more precisely, a super-app: primarily operating on mobile devices, WeChat defies the conventional notions of social media known by most Westerners. For example, in one of the earliest attempts to define social media, Kaplan and Haenlein stated, '[social] media is a group of internet-based applications that build on the ideological and technological foundations of Web 2.0, and that allow the creation and exchange of User Generated Content' (2010, p. 61).

Subsequent scholars continue to stress the feature of user-generated content as what makes social media distinctive from other medium forms or communication tools that can also be used for socialising (e.g. SMS). For instance, according to Carr and Hayes (2015, p. 50), '[social] media are Internet-based channels that allow users to opportunistically interact and selectively self-present, either in real-time or asynchronously, with both broad and narrow audiences who derive value from user-generated content and the perception of interaction with others.'

Is WeChat such an instance of social media defined by its function as a platform for user-generated content? Applying this Western idea, we would soon find something strange: as we shall detail Chapter 2, WeChat was initially was not social media but it gradually *grew into* one and then *outgrew* it. When first released in the App Store on January 19, 2011, its Chinese name Weixin meant micro-messages.[2] It was an instant audio messaging application – a cell phone walkie-talkie according to its self-description (Figure I.2) (http://bit.ly/2C4Nsmz). Many reviews at the time accused WeChat of copying Kik, Talkbox and WhatsApp – three widely-used messaging applications then. By November 2017, WeChat had accumulated 980 million monthly active users globally, increasing from 899 million the previous year (China Academy of Information and Communications Technology, 2017; Tencent, 2017b). WeChat is among the most popular apps used in China: 8 out of 10 Chinese smartphone owners use WeChat (Long, 2017).

Similar to WhatsApp, WeChat is mostly used for small groups and private communication among friends, family members and work-related contacts (China Tech Insights, 2017, p. 8) as opposed to 'the more public-facing platforms' like Twitter and Instagram (Harwit, 2016; Miller et al., 2016). WeChat users may share personal life moments, news and op-ed articles and content related to their work. They may subscribe to news and other topics of interest through a service called Official Accounts (similar to corporate accounts on Twitter), but they cannot use WeChat to create public groups or forums for communication with total strangers. It is therefore primarily a tool for private conservation like Facebook Messenger, although both WeChat and Facebook can create large-scale public influence through private and semi-private connections.

People also use WeChat for activities more than creating and sharing content. Eighty per cent of users reported having completed work-related tasks on WeChat such as sending documents and files, making transactions and having conference calls. In business communication, WeChat has a much higher penetration rate (90%) than email (less than 30%) in China (China Tech Insights, 2017, p. 12). In addition, third-party services keep growing on WeChat. Plugging into their WeChat accounts, users can order takeaway food, hail taxis, check-in for flights, book hotels, search nearby restaurants, pay utilities, enquire about their tax and social security benefits, start an online business, engage in in-store and online shopping, trade stocks and manage their wealth and the list goes on. In 2017, WeChat rolled out a service called Weixin Smart Transport that allows users to scan a QR code to pay public transport fares even without internet access at the point of transaction.

WeChat has grown into a mega-platform that has no equivalent elsewhere in the world. If you have never used it, imagine you could combine 'lite' versions of Facebook, Yelp, TripAdvisor, Priceline, Groupon, DealCatcher, Quora, TD Ameritrade and much more, and WeChat is the resulting combination. The aspiration to integrate add-on functions to app development is not unique to WeChat. Consider Google's many services – Google Reader for news, Google

Figure I.1. An Illustration of WeChat As An All-in-one App.

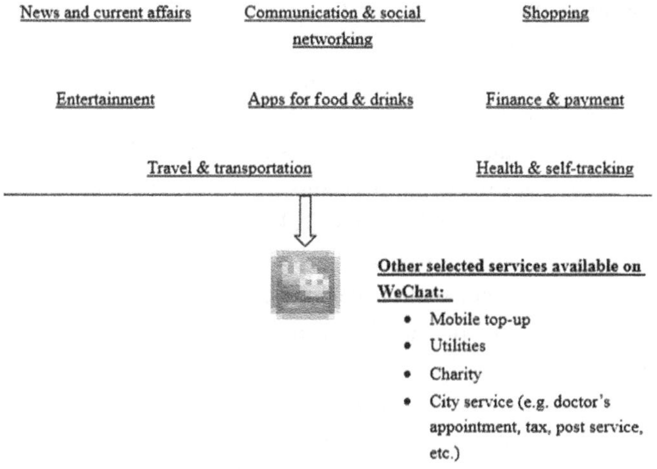

News and current affairs	Communication & social networking	Shopping
Entertainment	Apps for food & drinks	Finance & payment
	Travel & transportation	Health & self-tracking

Other selected services available on WeChat:
- Mobile top-up
- Utilities
- Charity
- City service (e.g. doctor's appointment, tax, post service, etc.)

Hangouts for social networking that replaced Google Talk and Google+. While some of those Google products achieved mediocre success or were discontinued, WeChat has outstripped them by developing into a one-stop gateway to more than 20 functions. The *Economist* named WeChat 'one app to rule them all' (2016). To many Chinese today, for example, senior citizens, using mobile internet means little more than WeChat. This unique capacity to grow and glue together an increasing array of activities marks WeChat as a mega-platform set apart from social media apps known to Westerners (**Figure I.1**)[3].

I.2. THE SUPER-STICKY WECHAT

WeChat is super-sticky because it includes so many functions and it keeps growing to the extent that its average Chinese users are glued to the meta-platform whenever they use their smartphones. In software development and interface design, one principle is to cultivate loyal users, to 'hook' customers (Eyal, 2014) or use 'sticky' design, because it tries to attract users permanently while preventing them from leaving the platform (Edelman & Singer, 2015). At its extreme, a sticky design turns into an addictive design (Schüll, 2014), which means a series of design decisions are made to stimulate and enhance addictive behaviours. Take casinos as an example. Anthropologist Natasha Dow Schüll found that the electronic gambling interface of slot machines, the interior lighting and floor plans, and the gambling ambiance, are all devised to entice gamblers to lose track of time so that they can spend as much time as possible in the casinos (Schüll, 2014). Digital products including gadgets like smartphones and software applications are becoming a fertile land for design tweaks and tricks that make them difficult to resist (Alter, 2017). The autoplay function on video streaming sites like YouTube and Netflix is one of the early designs for retaining viewers. The red notification dot showing the number of unread messages for social media apps and email apps is another example of sticky design. The goal is to lure users to tap or click on the app icon to enter and immerse themselves in the app-mediated world.

As far as retaining users and sticking them to the app is concerned, WeChat is probably the world's most outstanding case of sticky design. In fact, we see WeChat as *super-sticky*, because it aspires to create a gateway platform for its 980 million users such as Jay to carry out most of their daily business. Most importantly, users can access this wide range of services without switching between WeChat and other apps or web pages. As Jay implied in his comment at the end of the WeChat Sabbath experiment, they do not have to *leave* WeChat. WeChat is almost everything and users are happily stuck to the adhesive mega-platform. Many see their WeChat habit as such due to their own free will. Or so they think.

Connie Chan (2015), a partner at the venture capital firm Andreessen Horowitz, explained WeChat's approach. She wrote, differing from Facebook's business model of data-driven ads delivery, WeChat 'cares more about how relevant and central WeChat is in addressing the daily, even hourly needs of its users […] [It] has focused on building a mobile lifestyle – its goal is to address every aspect of its users' lives, including non-social ones.' Offering a space '[…] that allows [users] to easily connect with family and friends across countries' remains a core service of the app (WeChat, 2017). A new slogan 'WeChat is a lifestyle' was put to use from 2016 (Figure I.2). With those ever-growing functions increasing the

Figure I.2. Comparison of WeChat between 2011 and 2016.

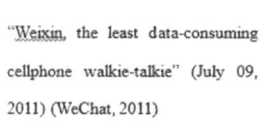

"Weixin, the least data-consuming cellphone walkie-talkie" (July 09, 2011) (WeChat, 2011)

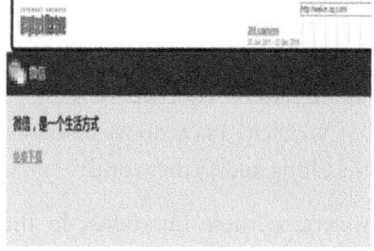

"WeChat, a lifestyle" (September 24, 2016) (WeChat, 2016)

Source: Internet Archives.

value of the platform exponentially – commonly known as the network effect, WeChat becomes central to users as well as service providers and content creators. This super-sticky platform is, of course, also a convenient one-stop site for state censorship and surveillance (Kessel & Mozur, 2016).

WeChat raises important questions for anyone who hopes to venture beyond the garden of Silicon Valley to explore the fertile grounds of Chinese social media, and to learn a few new things that enrich our understanding of digital platforms globally. You may wonder:

- How does WeChat work?

- How has it evolved both as a communication tool and as a socio-technical artifact?

- Why does it become super-sticky? Why is it able to weave itself into China's daily social fabric in ways hardly seen elsewhere?

- How can we understand this super-sticky platform in the contexts of Chinese society with its specific media practices, cultural traditions and political climate?

- What are the dangers in this one-stop site for social interactions and commerce, as well as surveillance and censorship?

- WeChat has been expanding globally – its wallet function (WeChat Pay) is now available in 19 countries outside China. In this context, what are the consequences of the globalisation of the model of WeChat? How do we assess its promises and pitfalls both in China and in the world?

This book presents our answers to these questions. In the remaining sections of this introductory text, we explain our approach to studying the stickiness of WeChat. We also demonstrate how studies on non-Western platforms like WeChat may contribute to our knowledge about social media and online environments in general. This chapter will end with an overview of the book structure.

1.3. HOW WE STUDY WECHAT

Social media is not so easy to define. Scholars, nonetheless, have studied the transformative impact of social media applications on people's media practices, social networking, political participation and activism (Bennett & Segerberg, 2012; Boyd & Ellison, 2007; Chakravartty & Roy, 2015; Gerbaudo, 2012; Lee, 2015; Rotman et al., 2011). They deploy different theories and various methods of studying social media, many of which inform our approach toward studying super-sticky WeChat.

The first set of ideas that we call 'platform studies' stress the technological properties of social media. For instance, the internet was believed to reduce the costs of organising a protest because information generally spreads faster and wider at a lower cost than through more established media like print or broadcasting (Earl & Kimport, 2011). This perspective of technological affordance leads scholars to define social media as a cluster of internet-based applications that share the attributes to foster peer-to-peer connections and content creation and sharing. Our earlier quote of Kaplan and Haenlei's (2010, p. 61) definition of social media as 'a group of Internet-based applications [...] that allow the creation and exchange of user-generated content' is representative of this perspective. Others also pointed out that social media allow 'formerly passive media consumers to make and disseminate their own media' (Mandiberg, 2012, p. 1). Social media users become prosumers because they create and curate online content by and for themselves while consuming media content.[4] Subsequent scholarly definitions elaborate on the means and purposes of user-generated contents. For Sloan and Quan-Haase, 'Social media are web-based services that allow individuals, communities, and organisations to collaborate, connect, interact, and build community by enabling them to create, co-create, modifies, share, and engage with user-generated content that is easily accessible' (2017, p. 17).

This framework of technological affordance draws people's attention to new patterns of user behaviours associated with the widespread adoption of the internet and digital platforms. It also offers scholarly vocabularies to describe the mainstreaming of a subtype of media and its cultures in a similar manner as for previous media forms such as radio and television. Despite the promises of the technological potentials, media practices are not *determined* by platform technologies. Take protest as an example, social media platforms usher in new 'logic' of 'connective actions' (Bennett & Segerberg, 2012) that boosts the spread of collective political actions because users personalise their media content and share it through their networks. Simultaneously, however, the rapidly growing momentum for protest is also a challenge with regard to ways of organising and sustaining the actions in order to achieve substantial outcomes (Tufekci, 2017).

Another perspective to understand social media sets its entry point of enquiry at media practices instead of platform or technological configurations. John Hartley went as far as to argue that '*social* media is a 'tautology", because '[all] sociality is mediated' (Hartley, 2017, p. 13, *italic* for emphasis). What matters in this line of enquiry is how users achieve, maintain and manage sociality when there are many choices of media and communication tools. Media scholars Madianou and Miller (2013), for example, developed the concept of 'polymedia' to describe the relationship between digital media, users and their social world. The framework of 'polymedia' treats social media as part of a larger system, rather than being discrete platforms, which together form an 'integrated structure of affordances' with many 'communicative opportunities' (Madianou & Miller, 2013, p. 170). The actual functioning of social media is therefore almost always 'in relation' to other means of communication and sociality. Because users exploit 'communicative opportunities' made possible by different media and communication tools in order to fulfil their real-life needs, this framework centring on media practices prompt us to examine what causes people to select different communication tools and how their social media usage patterns emerge.

The 'practices' perspective is rooted in the media studies tradition that sees media and society as mutually constitutive. It leads scholars to focus on how social and economic background and specific cultural contexts shape communication and sociality needs, which in turn gives rise to different cultural formations and media practices. For instance, internet cafes and family shops for affordable mobile phones flourished in urban China in the late 1990s and early 2000s because they satisfied the needs for communication, sociality and entertainment among millions of migrant workers (Qiu, 2009). Furthermore, moral and emotional investments in interpersonal relations also affect individuals' media behaviour. Studies have shown that teenagers were able to navigate a variety of social networking sites with considerable sophistication and develop complex understandings and practices of online friendship (Livingstone, 2008). When expressing their online identities and presences, they carefully calculated opportunities (for socialisation, friendship and intimacy) and risks (of privacy violation and the possible threat of abuse and so on) (boyd, 2014; Livingstone, 2008). Expanding the polymedia concept, Miller and colleagues (Miller et al., 2016) suggested that the choice of media platforms and what people do on them are essentially inseparable. In other words, '[s]ocial media should not be seen primarily as the platforms upon which people post, but rather as the contents that are posted on these platforms.' (Miller et al., 2016: 61).

The two perspectives outlined earlier are not mutually exclusive, and this book on WeChat benefits from them both. Specifically, the platform studies perspective informs us with regard to capturing and articulating the super-sticky character of WeChat, which sets WeChat apart from other social media platforms. We shall see that WeChat defines new 'rules of engagement' (Burgess et al., 2017) for its users, not only on the media platform per se, but also for their daily experiences in a much wider scope, such as booking flights, or paying at local business vendors. The platform mediates and sticks together many social and cultural activities that would otherwise be carried out more or less discretely. Using this approach, we are able to look into key social-technical objects on WeChat, such as Red Packet in the WeChat Pay function that has added new cultural meanings and social utility to a centuries-old cultural tradition in China – giving away money wrapped in red envelopes, now performed on a new digital platform.

We, however, do not treat the development of WeChat from a mobile walkie-talkie to a mega-platform as a natural process. The framework of media practices, in particular, leads us to examine the historical, cultural and social preconditions in China that have shaped the emergence and evolution of WeChat. For example, we trace the rapid ascendency of WeChat back to the earlier popularity of QQ, an antecedent social networking and entertainment platform also developed by Tencent, the parent company of WeChat. QQ remained China's largest social media platform until

December 2016 when the number of WeChat users surpassed that of QQ users for the first time (Tencent, 2017a).

Corporate software and platforms are notorious for their opaqueness — legal scholar Frank Pasquale used the term 'black box society' to describe the dominance of these secret and opaque corporate algorithms in our society (Pasquale, 2015). We examine the stickiness of WeChat as the outcome of complex social mechanisms involving users, interface design and Chinese social and cultural contexts.

To provide a comprehensive portrait of WeChat, we apply a multi-method approach (Denzin, 1989; Yin, 1994) to collect, triangulate and analyse relevant data. Our materials come from three major sources. First, we gather official statistics on the internet and social media usage such as those provided by China Internet Network Information Center (CNNIC). We also examine reports published by WeChat's holding company Tencent and the WeChat team.

Tencent is one of the most valuable publically traded company in Asia and in November 2017, it became the first Asian tech firm to be valued over $ 500 billion (Kharpal, 2017). We examine the company's financial statements, its stock price history, reports released by both Tencent and WeChat, as well as interviews and presentations done by WeChat employees or former employees. The rationale behind this is that understanding the business model of Tencent and WeChat will help us to grasp the complex and sometimes obscure and conflicting narratives around WeChat. The mindsets and aspirations of top executives (e.g. tech company founders) have a huge impact on the design of their products and the entire ecosystem that anchors on WeChat. As Marwick's (2013) study on the tech scene in Silicon Valley documented well, the social media metrics were designed by tech elites to encourage self-promotion, the effect of which trickles down to general users who pick up status-seeking behaviours and apply them to other social contexts.

Secondly, we focus on the various features and functions of the platform, including its historical versions, updates and services provided. We utilise WeChat app data retrieved from Internet Archive Wayback Machine and a third-party app data provider called App Annie. Wayback Machine is the oldest and largest Internet Archive that has accumulated cached pages since the early 2000s. App Annie is a private company that keeps track of mobile applications from both iOS and Google Play. We retrieve relatively comprehensive data about WeChat from App Annie covering its historical downloads, rankings and reviews of WeChat from its release in 2011.

Meanwhile, we document our own exploration of different functions on WeChat and deployed 'a walkthrough method' (Light, Burgess, & Duguay, 2016) to identify key logic of governance on the platform. The walkthrough is an experimental method that allows scholars to examine the intended users and the purpose of the platform as envisioned by its designers. Alongside this line of enquiry, we are attentive to differences between Chinese and English versions of WeChat including functions that were available in the Chinese version but omitted from or only permitted with restrictions in the English version.

Thirdly, we consult other secondary data and academic works about WeChat and social media in general. We are interested in people's daily activities and influential movements and events presented on the platform to see how WeChat users fulfil individual communication needs, mobilise for collective action, or use the platform for both purposes. For the topics on internet surveillance and censorship, in particular, we primarily draw on secondary sources (e.g., studies by the Citizen Lab at the University of Toronto). The book focuses on the character of WeChat and how it embeds into Chinese society. Therefore, although state surveillance and censorship is a built-in feature for all media in China with WeChat as no exception, we aim to extend our research focus beyond a censorship-centric lens.

Since the data are from different sources, we deliberately compare the patterns emerging from various sets of materials and identify consistency and inconsistencies among them in order to piece together WeChat's metamorphosis into a super-sticky mega-platform from 2011 to 2017.

1.4. BOOK STRUCTURE

This book consists of five chapters. This Introduction offers an overview of our goals, questions and perspectives. We identify WeChat's key feature as super-stickiness to describe both its historical development and its present all-inclusive quality. We also explain our basic approach and data sources.

Chapter 1 documents the chronological development of WeChat and positions it within China's long march toward a mobile society and within the coordinates of Chinese social media platforms. This chapter charts the political and economic conditions conducive to the success of WeChat and traces its inception back to the dominance of QQ and the making of mobile culture in China – to this day, QQ is still one of the most popular social media in China. WeChat began as the spinoff from QQ owned by Tencent. QQ's tremendous user base (700 million in 2011) gave WeChat an incomparable jumpstart. The ambition to create an integrative platform or media ecosystem initially experimented on the online system built around QQ and then passed down from QQ to WeChat as part of Tencent's design philosophy.

This chapter also compares WeChat with Sina Weibo and other popular social media and communication platforms in China, with respect to the user demographics, market share and stock price, media culture and platform functions. Overall Chapter 1 offers a sophisticated and historical account on WeChat, QQ and their holding company Tencent and their respective and collective roles in shaping Chinese internet and mobile cultures.

Chapter 2 explores and explains the benchmark functions of WeChat, highlighting Moments, Official Account and WeChat Pay (including Wallet and Red Packet). The chosen functions are emblematic of what WeChat allows its users to do for social networking, information dissemination and mobile payment. We argue that, together these functionalities reveal the accumulative construction of the app to become social, informational, transactional and infrastructural. We analyse the introduction, affordance and significance as well as the limitations of these functions. Through these key techno-social objects built into WeChat, we discuss the technical designs of these functions along with Chinese cultural traditions and some of the most popular social activities nowadays. This chapter shows that WeChat's growth and its super-sticky design builds on, mediates and expands popular communication and cultural practices in China. Gluing increasingly number of services onto the platform and straddling the online and offline world, in turn, enhance the accumulative and integrative trend.

Chapter 3 focuses on media activism and critical events on WeChat. The chapter presents three case studies on how different people use WeChat, namely, (1) Chinese American diaspora 'Supporting Peter Liang', (2) the deadly scandal of cancer hospitals paying Baidu for ranking, which was exposed by We Zexi's tragic death, and (3) the viral story about a female migrant worker named Fan Yusu. Facilitated by WeChat, these events either created collective memories or instigated social change. This process is by no means smooth or easy. Chinese government intervenes quickly in some cases but not others. Alongside this line of enquiry, we also examine how censorship operates on WeChat to contain activism on social media.

Tencent declares '[to] enhance people's quality of life through Internet services' as its core value (Tencent, 2016a) (See http://tiny.cc/85u6qy). In conclusion (Chapter 4), we assess the super-sticky design of WeChat considering Tencent's core value. We ask: what makes a good platform? What does it mean to enhance the life quality of social media users and to address their diverse needs – for users, for China, and for a global society?

NOTES

1. The opening story about Jay is from the short film on his 12-hour WeChat Sabbath experiment. The experiment was sponsored and conducted by WeChat Lab. It selected 6 people from diverse backgrounds and filmed their life without WeChat for 12 hours. The video of Jay's story is available at https://v.qq.com/x/cover/u1l082cs86frqom/e0023p4mnsb.html

2. The app changed its name into WeChat in 2012. In this book, we use WeChat throughout to avoid confusion and inconsistency.

3. The grouping of applications in the illustration corresponds to the categories in App Store. We created this figure based on one of the author's personal use of apps. The Figure only serves the purpose of visualising WeChat's inclusion of a wide range of activities that typical Americans or Europeans can only access through individual apps. The figure is by no means exhaustive or

representative of all users. The idea was inspired by Jessie Chen (2016).

4. The concept of prosumer first appeared in Alvin Toffler's *The Third Wave*. It went popular and became a signature of interactive online media that distinguished from previous media forms (e.g. print press) thanks to scholars like Alex Bruns (2009) and George Ritzer, Paul Dean, and Nathan Jurgenson (Ritzer, Dean, & Jurgenson, 2012).

CHAPTER 1

A SILVER-SPOON APP: WECHAT, TENCENT AND THE MOBILE REVOLUTION

Tencent's strategy is to build a platform. [We] welcome a variety of vertical businesses, such as gaming, information and communication, e-commerce, ISP, and IP telephone to develop on the platform, to create an all-embracing environment for applications. By then, QQ is an instant messaging tool that provides its users with many more useful business information. In so doing, QQ will become a 'golden platform.'
— Pony Ma, founder of Tencent, in 2001 (Wu, 2016, p. 116)

People have really gotten comfortable not only sharing more information and different kinds but more openly and with more people. That social norm is just something that has evolved over time.

We view it as our role in the system to constantly be innovating and be updating what our system is to reflect what the current social norms are.

— Mark Zuckerberg, founder of
Facebook, 2010 (Kirkpatrick, 2010)

1.1. INTRODUCTION: THE OLD DREAM FOR A MEGA-PLATFORM

One cannot fully understand the development of WeChat into a super-sticky platform without examining the history of its holding company, Tencent, and the role Tencent had played in shaping the mobile cultures and social media landscape in China before the rise of WeChat. Tencent's WeChat team, led by Xiaolong Zhang (also known as Allen Zhang), was located in Guangzhou, a city 80 miles from Tencent's headquarters in Shenzhen. The geographical distance implied a 'marginal' position of Zhang's team in the overall corporate structure of Tencent before WeChat's takeoff (Wu, 2016, p. 278). Indeed, Tencent had long been a giant tech company built on digital entertainment and social networking services before the inception of WeChat. The symbolic move of Zhang and his WeChat team from the margin to the centre of the Tencent Empire offers a unique perspective on the continuity and transformation in social media industry of China.

WeChat didn't start with a deliberate scheme to become a mega-platform, but it grew into one due to the combination of several key conditions. Not all these conditions have to do with a platform design, though as the next chapter will show, interface and functionality designs remain significant. Also important are pre-existing cultural practices and the media environment in China. Media scholars remind us of the significance of pre-existing cultural practices and socio-economic conditions in influencing the patterns of new technology adoptions and online behaviours (see for example, Miller et al., 2016; Qiu, 2009; Wu, 2014). Specifically for China's internet industry, a recent study shows that preceding vernacular practices among users for video spoofing and fan-subbing paved the way for the boom of the online video industry such as wildly popular live-streaming sites, video-sharing and commenting (Li, 2017). Although these popular user practices are often associated with the vast media piracy market in China, which may hinder scholars from recognising their constitutive roles, the momentum of users' habitual practices persist and shape the online video industry (ibid.).

Aligning with this approach, this chapter aims to tease out what cultural, technological and political factors contributed to making it possible for a super-sticky WeChat to rise and ripen. First of all, WeChat's expansive and super-sticky feature is not unprecedented. For anyone familiar with China's internet culture, Tencent was already a giant tech company built on entertainment and social networking services before the inception of WeChat. It has long been known for its aggressive expansion into new sectors – instant messaging, virtual community, news, music, games and so on – then integrating them all into its flagship social media product centring on an instant messaging service called QQ (Figure 1.1). Not only did the gene of super-sticky design pass from QQ to WeChat, QQ user base – 700 million when WeChat came out – but also its predominant position in Chinese social media market gave WeChat a jump start. In short, WeChat is a silver-spoon platform if we consider the extraordinary wealth it inherited from Tencent.

In China, as in most developing countries, internet connectivity depends mainly on the mobile phone, which leads to distinct cultural practices. Distinctive mobile internet cultures

Figure 1.1. QQ: The Prototype of a Mega-platform.

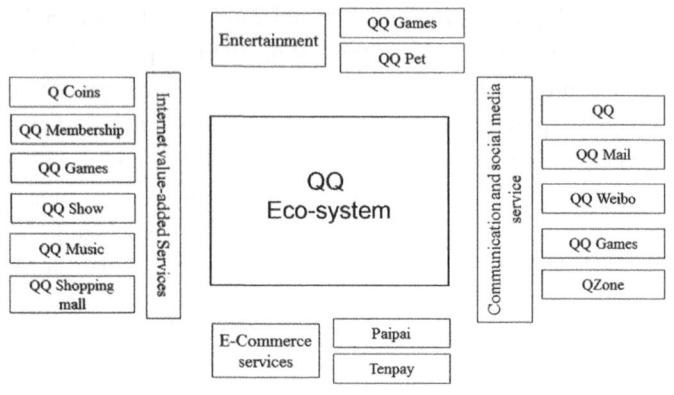

were conducive to the rise of both QQ and WeChat in China, the two products that have made invaluable contributions to the rise of Tencent as the most valuable company in Asia and its triumph over state-owned enterprise China Mobile and the e-commerce giant Alibaba domestically (Zhang, 2016). The following section first discusses mobile cultures in China and then positions WeChat within the business map of Tencent and in the broad political landscape in China. While comparing WeChat with Sina Weibo (Chinese version of Twitter) and other internet services such as MSN, we are also attentive to the shifts in the online public spheres that may have far-reaching implications for Chinese society and beyond.

1.2. MOBILE CULTURE IN CHINA: QQ, TENCENT AND SOCIAL MEDIA

Tencent was founded in 1998 by Huateng Ma (a.k.a. Pony Ma) and went public in 2004. The early years of the company were modest when it aspired to become an internet portal for pager service (China was the world's largest wireless pager market at the time) while emulating ICQ, by far the most popular instant messenger in the late 1990s. This could be seen in the name of its first product, OICQ, which was renamed QQ in 2001 because Tencent was sued for infringing the trademark of ICQ. By then, Tencent had formed a strategic alliance with China Mobile in the programme called Monternet (Mobile + internet). China Mobile was a recently founded state-owned telecommunication company, the dominant player in the mobile telecom market, and Monternet allowed ISPs and Internet Content Providers (ICPs) to partner with China Mobile and provide a variety of internet-based (or rather, wireless net-based) valued added services, such as WAP platforms and short-message applications. In March 2001 alone, more than 30 million messages were transmitted by mobile QQ via Monternet, accounting for more than half of the business volume of the latter (http://bit.ly/2FQtNEZ). Monternet, with QQ as the backbone booster, mainstreamed instant messaging as the main communication tool in China. By 2002, the total number of instant messages sent through China Mobile network reached 79.3 billion, while messages sent by Americans in the same year accounted for less than 10% of it (7 billion) (Wu, 2016, p. 68, 70). Tencent integrated QQ into Monternet and the collaboration brought Tencent its first goldmine: RMB 10.22 million (US$ 1.23 million) in 2001 (http://bit.ly/2tXq3A4). Monternet became the sole source of profit for Tencent in 2001 and continued to be a major source of profit until 2006 when the partnership was terminated by China Mobile. This means that QQ was much more than a copycat of OICQ due to its capacity to generate real revenues that could be used to support a full spectrum of R&D projects. More importantly, OICQ was designed for computer interfaces, whereas QQ was a mobile application from day one (Barboza, 2007).

How come Tencent could succeed in fostering QQ and a full range of QQ-based internet services, then basically replicate the process in WeChat buildup, which together contribute to Tencent's commercial success? According to Bloomberg, Tencent's stock market value reached US$ 528 billion in November 2017, surpassing Facebook whose valuation was $ 522 billion (https://bloom.bg/2FIRN17). The meteoric rise of Tencent as the superstar in Chinese mobile social media market in the first decade of the 21st century has to be understood in the context of China's working-class networked society (Qiu, 2009). Unlike Western countries, China is a large developing country. But unlike most other developing countries, China is rapidly industrialising into the 'workshop of the world'. It's also quickly urbanising with a thriving economy that depends categorically on low-pay labour provided by the rural-to-urban migrant population working for privately-owned companies. Against such social and economic backdrops, Chinese working people need inexpensive ways of social networking, entertainment and payment, which they can carry around.

QQ users were dominated by teens and twenty-somethings. In 2007, more than 70% of QQ users were under 30 years old and users under 24 accounted for nearly half of QQ population (Huynh, 2008). A typical QQ user then would be a 25-year-old who had finished 12 years of school but never entered college or university. She worked in sales for an insurance company; he was a janitor in the warehouse. Both lived in a coastal city of South China, earning a meagre monthly salary of RMB 600–800 (US$ 72–97), out of which they paid RMB 5 ($ 0.6) for unlimited QQ data service on their low-end mobile phone. The bandwidth was narrow and internet was slow, but it was good enough for text chatting and low-resolution photo sharing. Most important, QQ gave its users a precious sense of stability because they had to migrate from the countryside to the city, and from one city to another, following demands in the fluctuating job market. As a result, they had no stable mailing address and often had to change their mobile phone number every other year. The only thing that stays unchanged is their QQ number, a string of 5-11 numerical digits, which can be used to access dozens of QQ services through mobile and computer interfaces and can be used to access WeChat today, too.

Tencent, the tech empire, is known from the early days for its 'imperialist' tendencies to copy trending applications from others, improve them to better suit the needs of the Chinese people, and integrate them all into one mega-platform that used to be QQ (Tencent Ten Years Writing Group, 2008). Within QQ, one can send text messages to mobile phone numbers (QQ message), check email (QQ mail), listen to music (QQ Music), play games (QQ Games), join multimedia chat rooms, construct personalised decorated virtual space with uploaded photos and blogs (QZone), read news (QQ.com) and shop online (Paipai) and more. QQ supports instant voice, video and file transmission. It also develops new functions, including emoticons, image capture, file sharing and more (Figure 1.1). Most noteworthy is a standard in-system payment method introduced and made popular by Tencent – Q Coins. Users can purchase and transfer the virtual currency, and use Q Coins for virtual goods (e.g. clothes for QQ Show avatars, or wallpaper for QZone) or any type of paid internet value-added services offered by Tencent (e.g. paid membership for QQ Music). Q Coins inject fluidity into all functions and services available via QQ, circulating in the QQ system. The super-sticky WeChat of today resembles the mega-system of QQ in many respects, but one distinction between WeChat and QQ is the use of money. As Chapter 2 shows in detail, WeChat facilitates real money transaction among users whereas Q Coins are products Tencent sells.

QQ's tremendous user base (more than 700 million in 2011) has provided WeChat with an incomparable jump-start. By March 30, 2012, 433 days after its launch, WeChat's users reached 100 million. It took QQ nearly four years to complete the journey toward 100 million users, and four years for Twitter and five and half years for Facebook, respectively (Wu, 2016, p. 283). QQ took nearly four years to complete the same symbolic journey.

QQ and QZone remain the most popular social media platforms despite the rise of WeChat. QQ, in particular, has the largest number of users in China and kept growing until 2016 when WeChat (963 million) surpassed QQ (850 million) for the first time in a number of monthly active users (Tencent, 2017a, 2017b). Data from App Annie, a mobile app data aggregator company, shows that the early exponential growth of WeChat correlated with the integration of the platform with QQ. WeChat had a mediocre performance in the App Stores in the first six months after its release, as it never reached the top three in the category of social networking apps in China. It ranked second for the first time on May 26, 2011, after WeChat version 2.0 allowed for QQ email notifications. WeChat topped the list of social networking apps from June 10 to June 26 in 2011, after it added a function to add friends by searching QQ friends, QQ email contacts and phone contacts – an almost full access to QQ (App Annie, http://bit.ly/2DCSgMp). It fell back after its initial rise and maintained a steady place in the top two with intermittent rises and occasional falls since then. Many of WeChat's functionalities prior to WeChat Wallet overlap existing services available on QQ (Table 1.1).

Table 1.1 Comparing QQ and WeChat in 2013.

Functionalities	Mobile QQ	WeChat
Messaging	Yes	Yes
Audio/video chat	Yes	Yes
Group chat (including conference call)	Yes	Yes
People nearby	Yes	Yes
File transmission	Yes	Yes
Games	Yes	Yes
QR code	Yes	Yes
Socialising	QZone	Moments
Open platform	None	Official accounts

1.2.1. The Promise and Pitfalls of the Golden Platform

As early as 2001, Pony Ma, the founder and CEO of Tencent, envisioned the future of QQ in this way:

> *'Tencent's strategy is to build a platform. [We] welcome a variety of vertical businesses, such as gaming, information and communication, e-commerce, ISP, and IP telephone to develop on the platform, to create an all-embracing environment for applications. By then, QQ is an instant messaging tool that provides its users with many more useful business information. In so doing, QQ will become a 'golden platform'' (Wu, 2016, p. 116)*

None of this was first conceived at the company that was founded to transmit pager messages, but Tencent spotted them, saw their growth potential and made them part of the ecosystem under QQ, and later WeChat. The ambition to build a golden platform propelled Tencent and thus QQ and WeChat to hone its integrative capacity to meet different needs of a diverse body of constituents. A golden platform, if fully realised, would be embedded into users' lives, like electricity and water. Different from Zuckerberg's eagerness to connect people, Ma wants his Tencent (via QQ and WeChat) to create 'a new online lifestyle.' Tencent aspired to become the utilities for that new online lifestyle.

The rhetoric of building an online living system is a recurring strategic theme in Tencent's corporate documents. Take a look at their annual reports:

> *Tencent is aspiring to create a new mode of 'living online.' Just like people need utilities for everyday practice. Tencent wants to become the utilities on the internet,* offering one-stop internet service solutions *that cover the whole value chain.* (roman for emphasis, *Tencent Ten Years Writing Group, 2008, pp. 113–14)*

> *In 2014, we focused on our 'connection' strategy, linking our users with content, services, and hardware to* enhance their lives online and offline. *Leveraging our core communications and social platforms, Weixin [WeChat] and mobile QQ, we made significant progress in fostering* a healthy mobile ecosystem. (roman *for emphasis, Tencent, 2015, p. 6)*

> *Important changes can be achieved through connecting millions of internet users […] [Through]*

> *the* 'smart living' system *in QQ and Weixin/ WeChat, people and public services can be digitally connected, facilitating developments in transport, healthcare, environmental protection, public safety and other social arenas. (*roman *for emphasis, Tencent, 2017a, p. 88)*

This may appear like a shrewd business strategy, but in reality it brought major challenges to Tencent because it had to face one lawsuit after another from competitors claiming that Tencent had stolen from them and used its dominant market position as the basis for unfair competition, going so far as to break the law.

This is the underbelly of super-stickiness: every addition to Tencent's online applications ecosystem brings it a legal liability, whose cost can be very steep as the company learned from its loss of the OICQ brand back in 2001. Meanwhile, China is not known for its rule of law. It is, instead, an authoritarian country where judges, lawyers and the court system are all controlled by the Chinese Communist Party. Losing a lawsuit, therefore, would mean much more than a simple economic loss. It indicates political risk, too. Furthermore, Tencent has gained momentum from its partnership with China Mobile to develop its own QQ and a suite of internet value-added services, but it also had to grapple with the disadvantage of the symbiotic relationship of this kind. The huge success of QQ threatened the market share of China Mobile, which offers text message services. China Mobile as a state-owned telecommunication enterprise controlled the access to the information infrastructure and the Wireless Application Protocol (WAP). Once denied this access, Tencent faced daunting challenges and precipitating profit loss. Tencent's revenue plummeted in 2005 when China Mobile decided to limit its partnership with Tencent (Wu, 2016).

In the meantime, QQ suffered from overall negative news coverage and unfavourable public perceptions in the 2000s, as Koch and colleagues (2009) documented. This had to do with the fact that Tencent had grown so phenomenally, altering ways of life in China especially among the younger generation that worried parents, grandparents, teachers and the authorities. The pendulum of Tencent's participation in and exclusion from Monternet is symptomatic of the power relations embedded in the media ecology in China. The established political and economic system, along with interest groups (e.g. state-owned enterprises such as China Mobile), set parameters for how far a tech company like Tencent can develop and to what extent it may grow in terms of competing against the system. In the early 2000s, Tencent wasn't very effective with its public relations. The numerous lawsuits it had to face suggested that it had too many enemies in the IT industry and beyond. More than once, the company unintentionally stepped on the toes of the government, for example its Q Coins virtual currency that was deemed a threat to China's financial wellbeing by the Central Bank in Beijing. Q Coins enabled real money transactions — roughly one RMB equals one Q Coin. Though users are supposed to purchase Q Coins from Tencent only and peer-to-peer transactions are banned, the virtual currency practically operates outside and hence poses threats to the contemporary financial regulatory framework. Hacking and stealing QQ accounts proved to be a shortcut to accumulate Q Coins. Stolen accounts used to be a rampant nightmare for Chinese QQ users. The currency in the QQ world, however, has generated unexpectedly enormous revenue for Tencent. In the first half of 2006 alone, revenues generated from the sales of Q Coins contributed to 0.9 billion RMB out of 13 billion RMB made by Tencent (Yang, 2006).

Pro-government media and scholars raised security questions about the virtual currency and blamed Q Coins for facilitating online gambling. Even though the alleged gambling or money laundering activities took place on Taobao.com, the online marketplace owned by Alibaba, Tencent had to take actions to limit the circulation of Q Coins from the virtual to the real world (Sina, 2007; Wang & Wang, 2006). Tencent took the initiative by joining other big tech companies in China urging the government to make proper regulations around virtual currency and online game properties (Fowler & Qin, 2007). The Ministry of Culture and the Ministry of Commerce announced *Notice on Strengthening the Regulation on the Administration of Virtual Currency in the Online Games* in 2006 and The Ministry of Culture issued *Interim Measures for the Administration of Online Games* in 2010. Despite regulations by both the state and the company, Q Coins trading remains popular and the black market for QQ scams persists (Zhou, 2014).

High-profile events such as this occurred repeatedly. The result was that Tencent had no choice but to improve its relationship with the authorities. The massive attack on Q Coins met with no substantial resistance or alternative narratives from Tencent, and the lesson learnt from Q Coins controversy around 2007 foreshadowed Tencent's technological imagination and practice for designing a similar yet equally (if not more popular) functionality on WeChat – the WeChat Wallet, which generally keeps a safe distance from the existing financial system, embraces the financial measures to mandate all mobile payments to route through a centralised clearing house by the People's Bank of China (PBoC) (Hong, 2017), and aligns with political initiatives by the central government to develop a social credit system for Chinese citizens (Botsman, 2017). We will elaborate on WeChat Wallet in Chapter 2.

While the party-state shields the corporation from legal and political risks as well as foreign competitors such as Facebook and Twitter by upgrading the Great Firewall, Tencent supplies its data – from both QQ and WeChat – and becomes a central tool for the government's social control machinery (Harwit, 2017). During a tour in 2017 of the Online Public Opinion Monitoring Lab at the official *People's Daily*, one of us witnessed a dramatic wall-to-wall display of real-time surveillance data fed from WeChat. Tencent has the most Big Data, because it has the largest user base through QQ and WeChat due to its all-in-one products having so many functions that users would have a hard time leaving its virtual applications ecosystem. The same can be said about the Chinese government: without WeChat, without Tencent, could Beijing have such amazing access to so much social media data, so large in quantity, so detailed and so dynamically? The government, in this sense, is probably as much 'stuck' to the super-sticky mega-platform as WeChat users.

1.3. WECHAT'S ROLE IN BUSINESS MAP OF TENCENT

Regarding social media in China and in the United States, Christine Fuchs (2016) wrote:

> *Critical media studies envision a media and Internet landscape that is not ruled by capitalist and state power. This work has tried to show that U.S. and the Chinese 'social' media are not so different at all, but that rather both experience forms of capitalist and political control. (p. 36)*

Fuchs's assessment has wider bearings on the political economy of internet companies and their new shapes of media platforms in China, a society in transition with occasional clashes and collusion between an authoritarian government and a booming market (Jia & Winseck, 2018). Born in such a society, WeChat certainly is not exempt from the influences of capitalism and 'Big Brother,' as Yang pointed out, '[political] and commercial forces have penetrated deeply into cyberspace everywhere and China is no exception' (2011a, p. 1048). One must also note that political and capital forces do not impact equally and in the same manner on each online platform in China. To echo Yang's caution against the tendency to study the Chinese internet 'in isolation from its social, political and cultural contents and contexts' (ibid.), this section draws readers' attention to two nuanced aspects of WeChat. First, its design plays a unique role in the business map of Tencent in particular, and in the political map of the Chinese government at large. Secondly, regarding practices, people's usage of the platform may go beyond the design and engineered purposes intended by the designers, programmers and supervisors. This extended usage is demonstrated by different new media events happening on WeChat and will be examined in Chapter 3.

Generally speaking, Tencent's core business is marked by a significant shift from a heavy reliance on revenue generated from value-added service to a more diverse source of profits including a soaring revenue generated from online advertising. WeChat is a crucial catalyst product to facilitate this transition.

In *Tencent Ten Year* (2008), the autobiography of Tencent Holdings Limited, the writing group noted several turning points of the companies. One of the most important turning points was July 16, 2004 – the day on which Tencent successfully went public in the Hong Kong Stock Market. Goldman Sachs assisted with the initial public offering, and the authors talk about the reasons that Tencent sought an IPO in Hong Kong, characterising those motives as pure, ambitious and even caring.

> *If (Tencent) seek for chances in NASDAQ, the founders can earn more money. But Tencent does not look for a temporary high-valuation or earning some quick money. It aims for a sustainable development of the future development [...] More importantly, (to seek for IPO in Hong Kong) is for the interests of the employees of Tencent, since they hold stocks of Tencent.*

The above statement forgot to mention one crucial thing: Tencent's available options in markets for an IPO were limited in the beginning. A company registered in the Cayman Islands, Tencent's biggest investor (owning 50% of the investment) was an overseas company called MIH Limited (a subsidiary of Naspers, the giant media group in Cape Town, South Africa). This left little chance for Tencent to seek an IPO in the conservative A-share market in China. Hong Kong Stock Exchange is more liberal and open, and it welcomed Tencent with an IPO price of HKD 3.7. Initially, the investors and media did not show much enthusiasm. The scepticism might be reasonable, since Tencent – a tech company – and its services might remind them of the bursting of the 'Dot-com bubble' not long ago, from 2000 to 2002. Indeed, the local media coverage of Tencent was quite scarce when it entered the market, and some reports negatively reported on the early downturn of the share (http://bit.ly/2FlBKml). In 2018, the share price of Tencent reached HKD 400 – the highest price among all the listed companies in the Hong Kong market – and enjoyed over 80 newspaper reports per day in Hong Kong. The company consistently performs in the market, as evidenced by their numerous acquisitions and investments (mostly related to information technology firms or businesses), while also ensuring the growth of its two major sources of revenues: value-added services (VAS) and online advertising. Revenues from Tencent's VAS business increased from RMB 1.08 billion for the year ending 31 December 2004 to RMB 107.8 billion for the year ending 31 December 2016. The revenues from online advertising services increased from RMB 54.8 million to RMB 17.158 billion (Tencent, 2017a).

Considering the predominance of advertising revenue in Facebook and Google (98% and 87%, respectively, in 2017), it may be surprising when considering that online advertising has almost been an uncharted territory for Tencent. The product that helps Tencent to break the ground for generating advertising revenue is WeChat. Tencent's stock price chart attests to this shift.

The IPO and the first boost period of the company, from share price HKD 3.7 to over HKD 30 from 2004 to the end of 2010, respectively, seems to be counting on the success of Tencent's core platform, QQ. Millions of active QQ users become customers who pay subscription fees; other revenue sources include the virtual currency Q Coin, which is required for QQ's derivative products such as QQ Show (superficial profile features); online gaming; video watching and a music service (Tencent, 2016b). Meanwhile, Qzone (i.e. the QQ blog service and instant messaging service) contributed most to the revenues from online advertising. After WeChat's release in 2011, Tencent even suffered a minor setback in stock price during that year. The real surge of the share price started in the middle of 2013, from HKD 50 to over HKD 400 in late 2017. In each year's annual report, Tencent still lists QQ as its primary product before WeChat; VAS and online advertising are its major sources of revenues. Ostensibly, the business map of Tencent has not changed, and WeChat is like the icing on the cake. It's just another instant messaging platform, like QQ, but with some different designs and features.

The details in Tencent's financial statements, however, tell a subtler change in the picture. In 2004, online advertising contributed less than 5% of Tencent's revenues. This number surprisingly reached 18% in 2016. Tencent attributed the unusual surge to the WeChat platform:

> *Performance-based advertising revenues grew by 81% to RMB 15,765 million, mainly reflecting growth in advertising revenues derived from WeChat Moments, our mobile news apps, and WeChat Official Accounts. (Tencent, 2017a, p. 12)*

Why WeChat attracts more advertisers for Tencent? On its Q&A page of online advertisements, Tencent stated in a straightforward way that the heaviest users of QQ (i.e. the potential consumers of the advertisements) are the younger generations who were born after the 1990s, while WeChat attracts users in a broader age range (15–40 years), who have decent jobs, city lives and reasonably deep pockets (http://bit.ly/2CB3Eb2). Such differences may be caused by different platform designs. One of the most obvious differences between WeChat and QQ is their icons. QQ's icon feature, a cartoon penguin, is cute and fresh but may fall short of professionalism and seriousness. Compared to the QQ icon, WeChat's 'two dialog boxes' icon is neutral, neat and chic (Figure 1.2), which not only holds teens' attention but also attracts adults, the elderly and the professional elites to use the platform. To maintain WeChat, Tencent even abandons one of its most profitable part of QQ – namely, QQ Show – when designing accessory services associated with WeChat. QQ Show allows users to purchase virtual items

Figure 1.2. Logo for WeChat.

(e.g. clothes) for their QQ icon/avatar. The profile feature for QQ Show, though helping to bring in a fortune for Tencent, often appears to be superficial, childish and unsophisticated in the eyes of adults who also tend to accuse QQ Show of stealing money from children's pockets (http://bit.ly/2oiaT3m).

Tencent would not let go of the profits at their fingertips. A comparison between similar functionalities available on QQ and WeChat sheds light on how Tencent aspires to achieve more through WeChat. QQ also has a service for information dissemination and broadcasting (QQ Shuoshuo) and a service for socialising (QZone). Their equivalent functionalities on WeChat are Official Accounts and WeChat Moments (Chapter 2 offers detailed analysis on these two functions). At first glance, the pairs of QQ Shuoshuo and Official Accounts, of QZone and WeChat Moments look similar and almost identical. One can use either Shuoshuo or Moments to share a brief thought while using QZone or Official Accounts to write blog-length posts. Official Accounts differs from QQ Shuoshuo in its authority and formality, although later Official Accounts dedicated to humour and gossip were developed. Tencent invited various government departments, financial institutions, high-profile companies and experts from different fields to open Official

Accounts. Most of them were social elites in China. Tencent's strategy is inspired by its major competitor company, Sina, whose media platform Sina Weibo is known for its verified accounts usually of institutions, celebrities and scholars and other public figures. WeChat differs from Sina Weibo in its expansion into the market outside China, where WeChat has launched promotional media campaigns that invite social celebrities to advertise the platform and seek collaboration with local government and companies in setting up Official Accounts (Negro, 2017). Eventually, Official Accounts and by extension WeChat have helped Tencent shed the cultural baggage inherited from its QQ suite platform. People stopped viewing WeChat as an entertaining, energetic, yet unsophisticated social space such as QQ.

Entertainment and games remain important segments on WeChat. For example, there are many gaming-related official accounts. Playfulness is the feature function of Red Packet on WeChat and social games on WeChat are very popular (Wang, 2018). But Official Accounts help expand the reach of WeChat: first-hand government policy releases, commentary on finance and economy, sports game reports, medical knowledge distribution and critical thoughts on other numerous issues. The Chinese Embassy's Official Accounts become an effective and efficient communication channel for overseas Chinese in the event of crisis or emergency as well as in routine tourism. Currently, there are over 20 million Official Accounts associated with governmental institutions, agencies or officials. The more the governmental public service relies on WeChat, the more free work and value they contribute to the expansion of the mega-platform, day by day, post by post, which makes it even more popular and sticky among citizens from all walks of life, especially mature and better-off citizens who are QQ users but are not primary contributors to Tencent's profits (Huynh, 2008).

1.4. WECHAT ON THE POLITICAL MAP OF CHINESE GOVERNMENT

The transformative design and promotion strategy may help WeChat gain traction among Chinese people with higher social statuses, but why should they turn to WeChat instead of other alternatives, or rather migrate from other platforms to WeChat? To understand how Tencent's WeChat stands out from the crowd, we need to identify its major competitor. When WeChat was born, giant companies, including Sina, Microsoft, Yahoo!, Google, Baidu and NETEASE competed head-to-head to win the internet business in China by promoting online platform services. Among all those platforms, people may consider WeChat's major competitor to be Sina Weibo, despite the fact that Tencent has its own microblogging site called Tencent Weibo. Sina Weibo is a public microblogging site; WeChat is a mega-platform characterised by mobile and messaging practices (Chapter 2 elaborates on this point). The two platforms indeed share some similar functions. For instance, the posts on WeChat's Moments can be viewed as microblogs/tweets, while Weibo Message offers an instant messaging service. However, all those functions and programs are derivative, meaning they serve or supplement the needs of each platform's core business. If a user chooses one platform instead of another, it's probably because she or he has a preference for instant messaging (IM) over microblogging or vice versa. In many cases, the users keep both apps in their smartphones to satisfy different needs and purposes. Though WeChat and Sina Weibo are not exclusive of each other, as WeChat becomes increasingly sticky and inclusive of many other functionalities, it attracts users and affects Sina Weibo and other platforms negatively – for content creation alone the former has already confirmed a decline caused by WeChat (Negro, 2017).

In the IM market, the biggest threat to WeChat and its services was from MSN Messenger, whose holding company is Microsoft. MSN was launched in China in 2000. Microsoft entered the online media market of China with a huge ambition. To bring the ambition to fruition, it has not hesitated to obey the censorship rules of the Chinese government (compared with the withdrawal of Google from the mainland Chinese market). Also, to ensure its online business as appealing to the local cultures, Microsoft developed a joint venture named MSN China to have control over its services in China, and once even reached Sina for international cooperation in reaction to Tencent's dominance. Nonetheless, Microsoft's efforts proved to be less than effective. Its search engine, Bing, couldn't keep up with the Chinese search portal Baidu, and MSN Messenger and its IM services were replaced by WeChat and QQ. The observers wondered: were those failures technical or political? While Microsoft made compromises with the Chinese government, it seems the platform designs made a difference and mattered more to the Chinese user. In Bing's case, for example, its algorithm system was never as popular as Google's in China. People complained about Bing's awkward user experience especially for searching Chinese keywords. Even the search engine's name was regarded as indecent for the local netizens since the pronunciation of 'Bing' is homophony to 'being sick' in Chinese (http://bit.ly/1svQWVU). When Google retreated from mainland China, Baidu and its localised searching mechanism have easily taken over the territories left behind.

MSN's failure in China was more complicated. Long before WeChat existed, MSN Messenger was once representative of the white-collar class in China with most users over 23 years old and 72% of users had a bachelor's degree or above (Huynh, 2008; and bit.ly/2FDqvG7). The middle and upper middle class enjoyed the chic and concise design of

MSN's IM and email service, which they could not find in QQ. However, such preference was accompanied by complaints of unstable connections from time to time. By August 2009, these complaints had reached a point where MSN Messenger and Hotmail service were completely shut down in China. At about the same time, an earthquake hit East Asia, which broke the submarine telecommunications cable between Hong Kong and Taiwan (Starosielski, 2015). The break shut down the internet data communicated between MSN's server in the US and its Chinese users. White-collar workers were shocked and furious. Some of them tried for a full day to log into MSN Messenger but failed. 'Why didn't Microsoft move its server to China?' the local journalists asked outright. 'The crisis would not have happened if had done so' (bit.ly/2HR6s7R). Seven years later, the urge became an order, with the release of the *Cybersecurity Law of China*. Article 37 of the Law reads as follows:

> *Personal information and important data collected and generated by crucial information infrastructure operators in China must be stored domestically. For information and data that is transferred overseas due to business requirements, a security assessment will be conducted in accordance with measures jointly defined by China's cyberspace administration bodies and the relevant departments under the State Council. (bit. ly/2gXvZ3p)*

Now, an earthquake in the Pacific Ocean may not damage the internet servers located in China, but Chinese society is facing tightened censorship. *The Cybersecurity Law of China*, effective on June 1, 2017, evidences the government's tightening grip on internet content. The long observation period by the government of cyberspace, during which they made some compromises with Chinese netizens, ended after the Arab Spring in 2010. Shocked by the social media activism shown in the Arab Spring, the Chinese government decided the internet posed a potential threat to the authority of the Communist Party. They must keep the contentious and revolutionary cyberspace at bay.

Thus, the Chinese government wants more from the online platforms to fulfil their political map, not only to obey their rules in a passive way but also to do the censorship job *for them*. MSN, with its US based mother company, might be okay with the former for business reasons, but it could not do as well with the latter as Tencent did. To satisfy the government, the WeChat team has developed the keyword-filtering and keyword-censoring systems (Ruan, Knockel, Ng, & Crete-Nishihata, 2016) and when it comes to users' data it hands over the access to the Chinese government without blinking an eye. WeChat is no more or less subjective to China's online content monitoring and censorship than other media platforms. Machine-enabled detection and deleting and humans' manual labour to flag memes with rich cultural connotations that often escape computer scans apply to all media outlets in China (Lin, 2018). The failure of MSN Messenger and the rise of WeChat was, therefore, felt to be almost preordained structurally when in 2009, the mouthpiece of the Communist Party said, '[I]t's time to develop our own MSN' (bit.ly/2FDqvG7). If there were no WeChat, then there will probably be YouChat or TheyChat or another online platform to do the job – one that is locally based and willing to abide by the regulations, financially and politically.

1.5. CONCLUSION: SELECTIVE ALL-INCLUSIVENESS

WeChat evolves to become a one-stop platform for an array of services and functions, many going beyond media content generation – a definitive feature of media environment of Web 2.0 and social media (Jenkins, 2008; Mandiberg, 2012). Users can engage in everyday social interactions and entertainment activities, and at the same time get private and public services at their fingertips (e.g. booking rail tickets, making donations, etc.). With penetration of over 95% among internet users, super-sticky WeChat seems to have achieved what QQ was designed to aspire to but has not yet materialised – to be a golden mega-platform.

The chapter demonstrates that the success of QQ and WeChat and the rise of Tencent, in general, are attributable to the socio-techno and cultural conditions and political climates in China. Socio-techno and cultural conditions in China are characterised by the dominant use of mobile technologies and its associated practices that often keep their momentum from legacy technology or platform to new technology or platform. Political climates, however, are less predicable and thus poses constant challenges for private internet companies. Private internet companies in China, as represented by Tencent, rely on maintaining good terms with the government and state-owned enterprises to flourish, yet are involved in discursive competition in the public sphere with the government on one hand and in business competition in the market with state-owned enterprises on the other. This implies that an unspoken role ought to be played by a growing mega-platform WeChat and companies like Tencent – that is, they provide public services that are often not requested for their counterpart private firms in the Western context. Many services made available on WeChat, including booking a taxi, making a doctor's appointment, charity donations, not only make life easier for mobile internet users but also fill a vacuum in a country with a relatively weak civil society. These are representative of power and benefits that WeChat brings to its users' daily life, which, as we show throughout the chapter, in turn, makes the platform indispensable for the governance of the country. As a result, the growing list of services also includes serving the needs of the central government. An account on WeChat thus defies simplistic and binary characterisation as being empowering or depriving or emancipating or a suppressive tool.

Although the field of media studies has recently seen urges for more studies on non-Western platforms and social media practices – some may call it, alternative platforms, we refrain from naming WeChat as such. This book is not a study on 'alternative social media' – a term often used to describe a social media platform like Diaspora as the alternative to the dominant ones like Facebook and Twitter. In Couldry and Curran's definition of alternative media, the key feature is that it 'challenges, at least implicitly, actual concentrations of media power, whatever form those concentrations may take in different locations' (2003, p. 7). WeChat, however, does not fall into this category. Instead, it has consolidated massive media power and does little to facilitate alternative political formation. Far more than that, WeChat's super-sticky design amasses unprecedented power in finance, small business and social services, truly turning into a quasi-utility for 'the new online (mobile) lifestyle' in contemporary China. The change to everyday culture is transformative. Power relationship shifts in another direction, too. As we try to demonstrate in reviewing the case of Q Coins and Tencent's handling of its relations with existing regulatory framework, WeChat Wallet in a sense is more conservative than disruptive, protecting the established financial order instead of challenging it.

The socio-techno and cultural conditions expand on and from pre-existing practices, and the political wills of the central government are mighty yet volatile. The development of WeChat is hardly the only example that is influenced by the combination of these factors. In combination, the circumstances raise more and severer challenges for interested scholars to conduct nuanced studies on China's digital platforms and internet in general. In Yang's (2011a) assessment on studies about China's internet, he acknowledged the daunting challenge ahead, by writing, 'How these powerful interests will affect the 'contents' of the internet and how people will counter these formidable forces of power is a key task for future critical analysis. A view of 'contentful' technologies should help to produce thicker and more sophisticated analyses' (2011, p. 1048). As media technologies like WeChat start to branch out beyond the realm of media content, what concerns us is not only what and why people post on the platform but also what they do *with* the platform and how they do it. The next two chapters focus on, in a reverse order, what users can do with WeChat's defining functionalities (Chapter 2) and what and why users post on WeChat for different events and circumstances (Chapter 3).

CHAPTER 2

SUPER-STICKY DESIGN AND EVERYDAY CULTURES

Essentially WeChat is a tool. Our goal is to build the best tool on the Internet.

— a team leader of WeChat Open Course, 2018

2.1. INTRODUCTION

As we wrote this chapter in January 2018, WeChat was about seven years old, and its latest version WeChat 6.6 had been released in December 2017. Since its 1.0 version, there were more than 30 update packets, through which WeChat has grown from a messaging tool to a super-sticky platform. In Chapter 2, we lead readers to delve into the definitive features on WeChat, highlighting Moments, Official Accounts, and WeChat Pay (including Wallet and Red Packet). Before concluding the chapter, we also connect the pattern of development – the super-stickiness – shown in the three functionalities to WeChat's latest functionality: mini-program.

- Moments (Friends' Circle)[1]: a timeline function that allows users to post their social updates or share content of interests. Moments shows friends' updates in chronological order. Apart from privacy settings to hide one's own or friends' social updates, the settings for Moments also allow users to be selective about to whom (e.g. a predefined group of friends) they want their updates to be visible.

- Official Accounts: a service provided by WeChat to individuals, companies and organisations enabling them to interact with their audience and clients directly. Official Accounts are similar to the Facebook business pages, but they gradually become a quasi-standalone interface for the account administrators to disseminate information as well as fulfil routine service request through instant messaging. While the first functionality is essential for WeChat to become a significant channel for news and information, the second distinctive functionality of Official Accounts paves the way for WeChat to become an experimental field for business transactions.

- WeChat Pay: a mobile payment service available on WeChat. After linking their bank accounts and since July 2016, completing real name verification, users can complete money transactions for both online and offline shopping via WeChat Pay (provided that the business owners have also enabled WeChat Pay) and transfer money to their contacts on WeChat. There are two ways of initiating WeChat Pay — (1) sending the money in a message or (2) scanning the QR code generated for the WeChat account and then completing the money transfer.

The aforementioned functions (like many others available on WeChat) are not groundbreaking (see Table 1.1) when they first came out if one considers the examples of QQ, Facebook Timeline, and Apple Wallet – all predating the WeChat functions. The chosen features for the chapter, nonetheless, are emblematic of WeChat's expansion from a communication tool to social interactions, information dissemination, payment, and third-party development, which together contributes to the all-in-one WeChat platform as of today. Each chosen functionality represents a step further toward integrating more services and functionalities into WeChat, and in collective terms, they reveal the cumulative construction of the app to become social, informational, transactional and now infrastructural. WeChat's transformation is linked to its adaptability to diverse aspects of Chinese social, economic, and cultural worlds and its ability to glue them together. The stages are documented in chronological order, but the sequence does not suggest that later functionalities are meant to replace the previous ones. On contrary, the cumulative nature of WeChat amplifies the network effect and makes the platform super-sticky.

The following sections characterise the three functions on WeChat through three metaphors: (1) a social and visual walkie-talkie, (2) an informational and service bazaar and (3) a scanning and messaging wallet. The metaphor is a powerful cognitive tool because it defines one thing through another by drawing on the analogy between the two (Barr, 2003). Barr found that metaphors are widely used in the human–computer interface because invoking metaphors has a clear benefit of making it easier to '[explain] some system functionalities or structure by asserting its similarity to another concept or thing already familiar to the users' (Barr, 2003, p. 9). That's why, for instance, the recycle bin in computer operating systems not only has the name but also an icon that resembles an actual recycling bin. It's easy for people to understand the functionality of the bin on a computer desktop. The term platform is a metaphor, too, when used to describe social media sites to imply the latter as connector or facilitator for social activities (Gillespie, 2017).

Not using scholarly terms like interpersonal communication or public sphere, we decide to invoke three metaphors – walkie-talkie, bazaar and wallet, to explain WeChat to readers, especially those who have never used WeChat before, by relating it to these metaphorical concepts and their associated yet varying meanings and activities in daily practice. The focus on three features of WeChat, however, is not intended to essentialise what WeChat is. On the contrary, as Lakoff and Johnson (2003) argued, though humans' conceptual system is wired to be metaphorical, metaphors never work in isolation and the interpretations of metaphors are always subject to the context, at the individual as well as the collective level. How to use WeChat and what WeChat is to its users are context-dependent. While metaphors prove to be useful in bridging two different phenomena or things, they have limitations in obscuring the differences and inconsistencies (Gillespie, 2017; Lakoff & Johnson, 2003). Dividing WeChat's super-sticky features into three metaphorical stages attest to our effort to capture the complex and diverse aspects of the platform.

We are selective in featuring three services offered by WeChat, but there are a number of other functions that are also significant for the development of the mega-platform. For instance, People Nearby – a function inherited from QQ – allows users to search strangers in close proximity and add them to their friend list. Another example is Shake – an invention of a Japanese social networking app LINE – through which users can add new friends who shake the phone simultaneously regardless of the geographical distance between them. The two functions have served as a major boost to the adoption of WeChat in its incipient phase.

In addition, Game Center on WeChat is a popular place for users to play social games, of which some have attracted hundreds of millions of users (Wang, 2018). To give readers a more detailed and comprehensive overview of the add-on functions of WeChat, we compile a detailed timeline in the Appendix. The timeline documents WeChat's major functions that have contributed to the expansion of WeChat into a super-sticky platform.

2.2. A SOCIAL AND VISUAL WALKIE-TALKIE

One day in March 2000, standing at Tokyo's Shibuya Crossing – arguably the busiest pedestrian intersection in the world, media scholar Howard Rheingold was struck by an astonishing observation that thousands of people crossing the street or standing by waiting for friends were preoccupied with texting on their cell phones. They seem to be connected and engaged with people far away while navigating the urban space. Rheingold (2007) coined the term 'smart mobs' to describe how mobile technologies are used by strangers to organise and mobilise rapidly for collective action in ways never seen before – an emerging phenomenon at the turn of the millennium. This marks an extraordinary shift in the everyday use of the mobile phone because the early history of cell phone technologies concerns mostly with 'making voice portable' (Goggin, 2006, p. 19). For this reason, the year 2010 is considered a landmark moment in the United States because the use of mobile phones for non-talking activities surpassed calling for the first time (Wortham, 2010).

When WeChat claimed itself to be 'the least data-consuming cell phone walkie-talkie' in 2011, it seemed to fight the tidal wave of popular instant messaging (IM) among Chinese by bringing the voice back. Chinese mobile phone users, like their counterparts in Japan, are frenetic text message senders. Since IM was introduced in China in 1998, the number of messages sent in 2000 surpassed one billion. In the next decade, the growth rate of text messaging continuously outpaced that of mobile phones. The number of texts sent skyrocketed nearly 19 times to 18.9 billion in 2001, which continued to grow to 90 billion in 2004 and reached its peak of 9 trillion in 2012 (People.cn, 2015). The decline is partially caused by applications like QQ and WeChat which allow users to send a text within apps. The trend in China corresponds to the global rise and decline of IM offered by telecommunications companies after mobile phones became the converging technology for a growing number of applications other than talking and texting, thanks to the success of the iPhone and the subsequent popularity of smartphones.

WeChat was not the only app to offer IM services in 2011. Among others in China's domestic market were its technological sibling QQ, Sina Weibo and Mi Talk – an IM tool developed by the tech company Xiaomi. The walkie-talkie WeChat that allows for a one-minute (maximum) voice message has been gradually developed into a daily communication practice among users, coming very close to the pervasiveness of text messages (Figure 2.1). Traditional telecommunication companies were facing a tremendous threat. China Mobile, the largest wireless service and IM service provider in China, reported a 30% shrink in its IM business volume in the third quarter of 2012, facing a staggering loss of one billion RMB (approx. $ 159 million) (Yuan, 2013). By 2013, among 300 million WeChat users, 91.8% send text messages to chat with each other while 90.4% send voice messages, both surpassing that of checking social updates on Moments (China Internet Network Information Center, 2013, p. 21). In July 2012 and February 2013, WeChat introduced services for video call and live group chats respectively. Chatting via text and voice

Figure 2.1. User Interface for Voice Messaging (Screenshots by Authors).

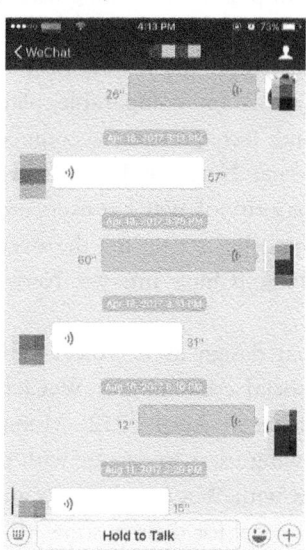

messages have topped the list of most popular activities of WeChat users ever since (China Internet Network Information Center, 2014, 2016b, 2017b). As of September 2017, 38 billion text messages and 6 billion voice messages were sent through WeChat on a daily basis and users spent about 140 minutes on average in 19 voice or video calls per month (WeChat Moments, 2017).

Reviving oral conversation on mobile phones seems to represent a reverse trend for observers who find 'text-based communication has largely replaced the voice-based use of the phone' (Miller et al., 2016, p. 2). But it proves to be successful for WeChat to become an essential and effective walkie-talkie, making voice-based phone communication popular again in China, where entering Chinese characters on the mobile interface may not be convenient for everyone. This initial design had an impact on the user demographics. In 2013, with equal popularity among users between 20 and 29 years old, WeChat had the largest portion of users over 30 years old (40%) and the lowest proportion of teenage users (8.7%) whereas on comparable platforms like Sina Weibo and QZone, teenage users accounted for more than 10% (China Internet Network Information Center, 2013). Nowadays, the majority of WeChat users are 30 years old or above, but the opposite is true for the overall social media population in China (China Internet Network Information Center, 2017b).

WeChat's initial design as a (voice) messaging tool also impacts on the social communities WeChat fosters after it introduced Moments in April 2012. Moments is the main functionality allowing users to engage with posting and sharing social updates with WeChat contacts and it allows users to set the visibility level for their postings (Figure 2.2). Miller and colleagues (2016) characterise WeChat as being a private-facing platform, which means it tends to enhance existing social bonds and encourage social interactions based on existing strong ties in one's social networks. The two most common ways to add new contacts on WeChat are (1) to scan the unique account QR code generated by WeChat (a service introduced in December 2011), and (2) to search specific WeChat ID, QQ ID, or one's phone number. Strangers are very difficult to find and add as WeChat contacts except using the Shake function, another evidence of WeChat favouring connections among trusted and personal contacts. From the beginning, existing social networks dominate one's WeChat contacts. Among earlier adopters of WeChat in 2013, the chance for friends and classmates to be a user's WeChat contacts is more than 90% and the respective chance for co-workers and families/relatives *and* teachers

Figure 2.2. User Interface for Moments (Left) for Social Updates and Select the Targeted Sharing Audience (Right) (Screenshots by Authors).

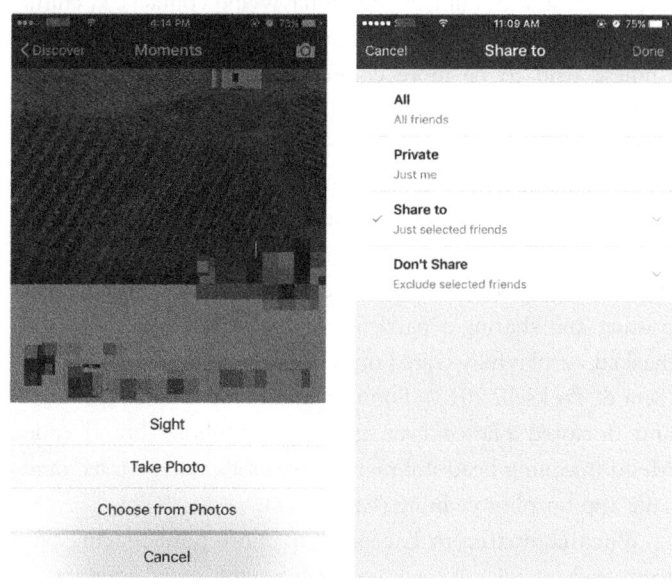

and supervisors at the workplace to be added onto WeChat contacts list is above 80% and 50% (China Internet Network Information Center, 2013, p. 21).

Moments is a pro-visual design for social sharing (Wang, 2016). It appears that users have to include at least one picture in their status updates before they can type any text (Figure 2.2). Pure text social sharing is so discouraged by the platform design that most people are not even aware that they can post text-only updates on Moments, let alone know how to do so (ibid.). Consequently, WeChat users are far more active in posting photos than Sina Weibo users, though users of both social media platforms are equally interested in sharing textual social updates (China Internet Network Information Center, 2017b). The discordancy in photo-sharing (especially selfies) can be explained by the fact that WeChat contacts have a higher level of trust and intimacy than Sina Weibo contacts. A culturally informed understanding of privacy leads one to believe that Chinese tend to be more comfortable about sharing photos on WeChat than on Sina Weibo (Seta & Proksell, 2015).

WeChat's later functionalities for six-second video clips sharing (Sight) and photo editing services for posts enhance its original pro-visual design. Precisely because of the high level of trust and intimacy, along with a controlled level of visibility, WeChat has given rise to the vernacular cultural practices of posting and sharing a particular genre of selfies – those with masked, or playfully edited or perfectly doctored faces or poses (Seta & Proksell, 2015). Popular cultural obsession with selfies and doctored photos even generated a phone brand called Meitu (meaning beautiful picture) that sells solely on its namesake app for photo editing (Fan, 2017).

When compared to Facebook or more public-facing platform such as Sina Weibo and QZone, the social interactions allowed on Moments are limited. One can either 'Like' or 'Comment' with a text-only reply to a friend's Moments. No public messaging or geo- or photo-tagging are available on Moments. In fact, one can only view mutual friends' engagement with the same posting (e.g. their comments), but not strangers'. This design grants more control to users over the content in their social media space and reduces the possibilities of publically contentious and embarrassing engagement (Miller et al., 2016). The high density of strong ties on WeChat contacts also places moral concerns on users' choices for what to post and with whom they should share the posts in the first place (McDonald, 2016).

Though empirical statistics support the characterisation of WeChat as a more private platform with a high level of controlled privacy and visibility and a low level of anonymity or unwanted interactions, recent popular users' behaviours demand more tweaks to the platform design. Given its high rate of overlap with existing close social ties (97.4% in 2016) (China Internet Network Information Center, 2017b), WeChat contacts have seen declining growth rates, even becoming stagnant among the middle-aged and senior citizens (China Tech Insights, 2017). For others, new contacts are most likely to be found in one's workplace (China Tech Insights, 2017). Tech industry observers consider it a shift of WeChat moving toward cultivating weak ties in one's social networks (China Tech Insights, 2017).

Hence, WeChat has become increasingly a communication tool for work. Statistics show that WeChat group becomes the primary channel for work communication in all tiers of Chinese cities and 80% of users use WeChat to complete work-related tasks like coordination and announcements (China Tech Insights, 2017). Though QQ mail has the highest penetration rate in China because it is associated with one's QQ account, text messaging, fax, and phones outperform institutional email as work communications in general (China Tech Insights, 2017). This communication pattern is not a coincidence but rooted in a historical pattern of Chinese mobile communication practices (see Chapter 1). Email as a communication tool has never gained a comparable foothold in China as it has in developed countries like the US. Prior to the rise of WeChat and in 2007, nearly 70% of Chinese internet users relied on instant message for communication rather than email (55%), while in the US only 30% of internet users used instant communication but more than 90% of them used email (Huynh, 2008).

The popularity of WeChat used for work blurs the line between social media interactions and work communications, and thus helps consolidate the informational services for both social and business activities on the platform. WeChat's beginning as a social and visual walkie-talkie does more than bring the voice back to mobile messages and foster pro-visual yet interactivity-constrained social sharing. Acquiring both social and business-oriented characteristics, WeChat also transforms what messaging can do as a type of user interface for subsequent functions like Official Accounts.

2.3. AN INFORMATIONAL AND SERVICE BAZAAR

Official Accounts is a service provided by WeChat to individuals, companies and organisations to interact with their audience and clients directly. Official Accounts is similar to Facebook business pages or Twitter corporate account, but they gradually become a quasi-standalone interface for the account administrators to disseminate information as well as fulfil routine service requests through instant messaging. It was first called Public Accounts and was released at the same time as Moments, but WeChat 5.0 renamed Public Accounts as Official Accounts in August 2013 and divided them into two types: Subscription and Services Accounts (Figure 2.3). The difference between the two types is concerned with information immediacy and interactivity between Official Accounts administrators and their followers. All Subscription Accounts are collapsed into one folder in the list of chats on the main user interface (Figure 2.3). They are unable to send push notifications to subscribers but they allow for new content to be published every two days. Service Accounts, on the other hand, can send push notifications to their subscribers. Newly available content will appear in the list of new messages like the new messages from contacts, instead of folded together like Subscriptions. Service Accounts also allow for more customisation for the user interface layout and hence more interactivity and the possibility for business transactions

Figure 2.3. WeChat Main User Interface (Left) and Unfolded List of Official Accounts Subscriptions (Right) (Screenshots and Annotated by Authors).

but these come at the cost of fewer quotas for publications of the new content (four times/month).

When introducing Official Accounts to the public in 2013, WeChat team claimed that 'every Official Account is an app' (Tencent, 2013). The functionality plays a major role in advancing WeChat's capacity to meet the diverse needs of its users for sociality, information, service and business. There are now more than 10 million daily operating Official Accounts and 3.5 million monthly active Official Accounts on WeChat and 57.8% of WeChat users are reported to have followed Official Accounts (China Academy of Information and Communications Technology, 2017; WeChat Moments, 2017).

Apart from carving out a more business-oriented domain, the separation of information and socialisation in the design of Moments and Official Accounts sets WeChat apart from

Facebook and other social media platforms which tend to mix promoted contents or ads with the threads of social updates. Finn Brunton (forthcoming) argues that the separation design allows for the flow of information in the messaging mode which 'renders [subscriptions] more distinct by keeping them in the main flood of messages and separate from Moments, which is for intimate social activity alone and has no branded company or media content, auto-posts from games, and similar clutter.' As Chapter 1 shows, selling targeted ads in the social media space has never been the major source of revenue for Tencent. The separation of Official Accounts content from Moments, of information-oriented Subscription from Service accounts, also suggests that WeChat pre-classifies the information streams and services *and* designs different outlets on its platform for each of them while brokering content and services for its exponentially growing user base.

Media interaction via Official Accounts differs from communication among contacts and socialising on WeChat in that it is heavily text-based. Brunton (forthcoming) goes so far as to single out the centrality of texting as the defining mode for interactions on WeChat, or in his term, 'chatification.' Indeed, texting dominates the interactions, or lack thereof, between users *and* service and content providers on Official Accounts.

Take China Southern Airlines as an example, which represents early adopters of WeChat Official Accounts. It launched two Service Accounts in early 2013 with a delegated marketing team. On China Southern Airlines Official Accounts, users can not only book flights and check-in, but also select seats, monitor flight status and check the weather in the destinations (Figure 2.4). More than a dozen customer services are provided via texting to Official Accounts. China Southern Airlines, later on, made more than 200 products available for sale through its Official Accounts. In its two years of operation by the end of 2015, China Southern Airlines' Official

Figure 2.4. China Southern Airlines Official Accounts User Interface (Above) and Seat-Selection Service (Right).

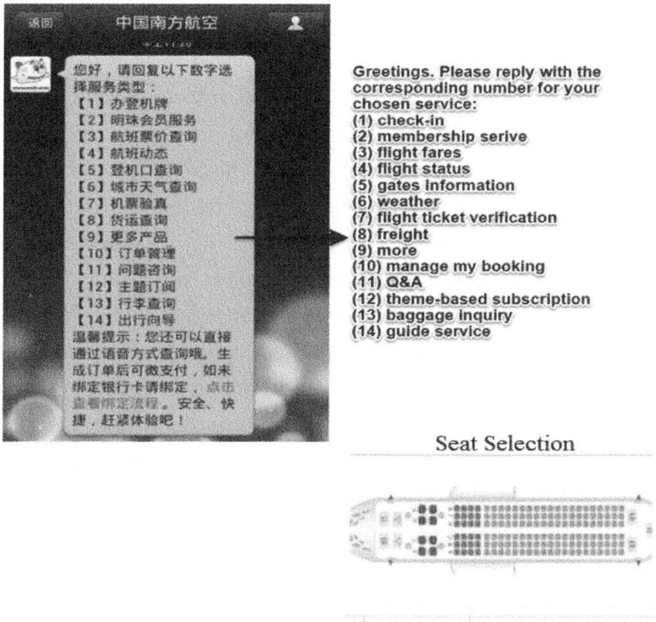

您好，请回复以下数字选择服务类型：
【1】办登机牌
【2】明珠会员服务
【3】航班票价查询
【4】航班动态
【5】登机口查询
【6】城市天气查询
【7】机票验真
【8】货运查询
【9】更多产品
【10】订单管理
【11】问题咨询
【12】主题订阅
【13】行李查询
【14】出行向导
温馨提示：您还可以直接通过语音方式查询哦。生成订单后可微支付，如未绑定银行卡请绑定，点击查看绑定流程。安全、快捷，赶紧体验吧！

Greetings. Please reply with the corresponding number for your chosen service:
(1) check-in
(2) membership serive
(3) flight fares
(4) flight status
(5) gates information
(6) weather
(7) flight ticket verification
(8) freight
(9) more
(10) manage my booking
(11) Q&A
(12) theme-based subscription
(13) baggage inquiry
(14) guide service

Seat Selection

Accounts had enjoyed more than eight million followers and both its mobile sales and WeChat mobile sales grew threefold from the previous year (CIW team, 2016).

The example of China Southern Airlines' Official Accounts illustrates how WeChat 'chatify' customer services, to expand from Brunton's idea (forthcoming). WeChat Official Accounts offers easy access to service providers and content creators to connect with their clients and a possible wider user base. Government agencies and public service sectors like a library, state mouthpiece like *People's Daily*, independent media content creators, as well as self-employed small e-commerce business owners alike, see great potential in WeChat. Instead of developing their own apps, institutions and individuals turn to WeChat Official Accounts. WeChat has become the most widely used platform among marketing teams in China's business world, with a penetration rate of 75.5% in 2016, much more popular than corporate websites (54%) or apps (31%) of their own (China Internet Network Information Center, 2017a). A similar pattern is found in internet users' access to government information and affairs. Since 2016, WeChat Official Accounts has become the most frequented place for Chinese internet users to access public service information, more popular than government websites and Sina Weibo accounts (China Internet Network Information Center, 2016a). Since WeChat Pay (next section) integrated public services like paying taxes and utilities and postal services, 4.5 out of 10 Chinese internet users rely on WeChat as the primary source for government affairs and public services (China Internet Network Information Center, 2018).

In short, Official Accounts don't just 'chatify' customer services, they appify and partially automate the work of communication and services for users and join them together on WeChat. With Official Accounts, WeChat becomes more than a one-stop information platform, it turns into an informational and service bazaar where users can get information and a variety of services at their fingertips. The initial breaking into business transactions on Official Accounts precipitated the mobile payment service on WeChat.

2.4. A MESSAGING AND SCANNING WALLET

2.4.1. The Glue of a Virtual Wallet

Since August 2013, users in China can link their debit or credit cards to their WeChat accounts through the Wallet function. Today, more than two-thirds of the Chinese mobile internet users use their phone instead of cash when shopping (China Internet Network Information Center, 2018). In the midst of China's phenomenal march toward 'cash-free society' (Aldama, 2017), WeChat Pay becomes the most noteworthy in the media spotlight. According to iResearch, an online market research firm in China, the total money transaction made through mobile phones in 2016 reached 58.8 trillion RMB (US$ 9 trillion), which is about 80 times larger than that of the US market (Knowledge@Wharton, 2017). The transactions in the first half of 2017 were close to 50 trillion RMB (US$ 7.7 trillion) (iResearch, 2017).

WeChat Pay's most well-known function is perhaps the Red Packet (or Red Envelope), which made a sensational debut in the 2014 Chinese New Year Gala of China Central Television (CCTV). That evening, for every minute during peak time, WeChat Pay had more than 4.8 million participants and 25,000 envelopes opened during its 'New Year Red Envelope' scheme. Two years later, on Chinese New Year's Eve in 2016, more than 2.3 billion Red Packets flooded through WeChat, and the number skyrocketed to 14 billion on Chinese New Year 2017 (China Academy of Information and Communications Technology, 2017). 'Sending WeChat Red Packet' has now become a routine activity for users all year round.

The immense popularity of Red Packet cannot be separated from an old cultural tradition in China and a more recent trend related to mobile phone use patterns. Traditionally, Chinese people distribute 'lucky money' among family members during the New Year celebration.[2] Money wrapped in red envelopes – a symbol of good fortune and best wishes – is handed by senior members of the family to younger ones (infants to unmarried twenty-somethings) and from grown-up adults to their parents and senior relatives.

The traditional red envelope money has taken on a digital life since 2014. WeChat's Red Packet becomes a 'digital extension of tradition' and redefines the tradition by adding a playful and participatory entertaining feel to it (Park, 2016, p. 19). For instance, scrambling for lucky money in WeChat private groups (e.g. the extended family group) becomes a common entertainment activity within groups and in social gatherings, making the long-term cultural tradition fun. One participant in Park's (2016, p. 22) study describes the experience: 'People throwing, for example, one hundred dollars in one WeChat circle of twenty friends, and everybody you know click on that red wrapped, red money, to see how much they can get out of that […] So, everybody can participate and people call it scrambling for red money.'

Messaging Red Packet money (Brunton, forthcoming), as WeChat allows users to do, also extends from a more recent trend – the pervasiveness of texting among Chinese mobile phone users. From 2000 onward but prior to WeChat, New Year greetings had already been mediated by mobile phones in the form of texting, which was already very popular as discussed in Chapter 1. Chinese New Year has been the busiest time of the year for texting. For example, during the New Year holidays in 2005 alone, 393 million Chinese mobile phone users have sent more than 12 billion New Year Greetings text messages – 31 messages per person. A reporter from Xinhua News Agency (2006) quoted an interviewee then complaining about texting and resending wishes as 'industrialising' New Year greetings. China has continued breaking the previous year's record of New Year Greetings text messages until 2012. After WeChat came out, the Chinese started to experiment with an audio message or video chat to express New Year greetings. The number of WeChat Red Packets sent on Chinese New Year's Eve 2017 reached 14 billion, comparable to that of text messages sent as New Year greetings back in 2005. The popular practice of sending greetings and wishes for the New Year remains, but the medium Chinese people chose to use has changed.

Situated against the cultural underpinnings of lucky money and the historical trajectories of mobile phone practices, WeChat's Red Packet extends the trend of mediating cultural practices to celebrate Lunar New Year and express gratitude and wishes to each other. The distinctive feature on WeChat lies in the fact that it offers an opportunity to integrate wishes and lucky money together in the form of messaging, as opposed to separating New Year greetings in IM and lucky money in the paper red envelopes. In short, expanding on Brunton's discovery, we argue that WeChat creates a messaging wallet for its users – meaning that both Red Packet and messages can be the carriers of money in the chat box (Figure 2.6).

Another popular practice that WeChat Pay appropriates concerns the use of QR (quick response) code. Ten months after its initial release in December 2011, My QR Code on WeChat was introduced to allow users to codify their WeChat account information into a picture of a matrix barcode (QR Code) ready to be read by a simple and quick scan by any smartphone. The picture of My QR Code can be shared in messages, too. Thus scanning My QR Code is a more convenient way to add new contacts than searching for WeChat ID.

A QR code reader is embedded in WeChat in a menu item called Scan QR Code. Scan QR Code is available 1) on the top right menu at the main WeChat interface (Figure 2.5) and 2) on the page after one clicks Discover on the main WeChat interface. The built-in QR code reader has significantly reduced the barriers for WeChat users to adopt the technology. After WeChat Wallet was available, scanning to pay became one of the two most common ways of money transfer on WeChat (Figure 2.6).

Figure 2.5. WeChat Wallet Interface.

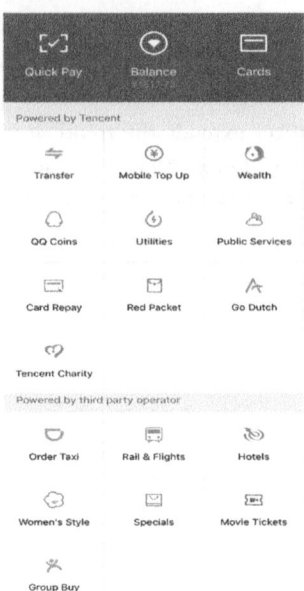

Scan-to-pay allows WeChat users to complete transactions without being on each other's contact list, which, as discussed earlier, is dominated by people one already knows. As Hart (2007) pointed out, money acquires the quality of both being impersonal and personal, which facilitates the exchange of commodities (values) and hence enables the market economy to flourish and simultaneously allows humans to attach and create a wide range of personal and symbolic meanings associated with money. While messaging money (including wishful and playful Red Packet) implies close affinity and personal aspects of the social relations, scan-to-pay permits the impersonal business transactions to take place on WeChat.

Super-sticky Design and Everyday Cultures 67

Figure 2.6. A WeChat Wallet That Can Scan (Above) and Message Money (Below).

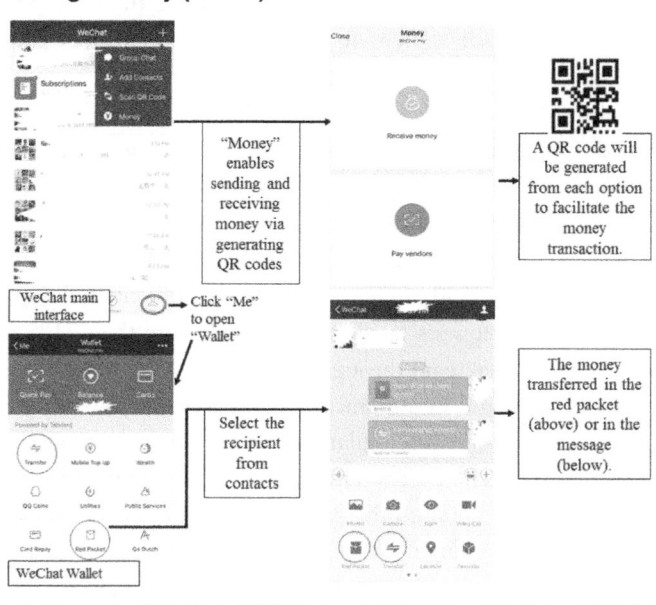

Payment helps to grow WeChat from being informational and social to transactional. Users are now connected to an array of services, online and offline, through WeChat Wallet, which is either offered directly by WeChat or by third-party service providers, including mobile top-up, transportation, movies, and so on (Figure 2.5). Even hawkers selling cheap vegetables in the street accept WeChat payments. As such, WeChat becomes a gateway to a full range of goods and services, and with the payment function, people can complete business transactions without leaving WeChat. This leads scholars to conclude that 'WeChat has gone far beyond a social media tool. It has the potential to become a highly hybrid mobile and social commerce platform [...] and much more' (Wang, 2016, p. 47).

Take Didi Chuxing as an example.[3] Didi is the monopoly ride-hailing app in China. In its early development, it took advantage of the transactional platform WeChat by joining the list of third-party service providers in WeChat Wallet. On the first day of listing, more than 20,000 ride requests were made through WeChat and 40% of them were paid via WeChat Wallet (https://goo.gl/ZrCqt1). This is indicative of how WeChat builds an app-within-app model. By 2014, when Didi had more than 100 million users from 400 cities, among 5 million ride requests facilitated by Didi, more than 71% of the ride fares were paid through WeChat Pay (China Academy of Information and Communications Technology, 2014).

Allowing money to circulate in the WeChat platform also means users can express more social meanings through money as well. Among others, users can easily make Peer-to-Peer (P2P) donations on WeChat. The sick, the poor, disadvantaged minorities, and other vulnerable groups can use WeChat to publicise their stories for the purpose of fundraising. Tencent Charity had used its WeChat Wallet function to help to raise over 3 billion RMB ($ 475 million) by March 2018 (http://bit.ly/2pruXA5). We will also discuss the charity service of WeChat in Chapter 3. The money floating through Red Packet and messaging may flow back to services, business transactions, and micro-donations, meeting the social, professional, and material needs of WeChat users.

2.4.2. The Tipping Dispute: An Epitome of the Clashes of Platform Infrastructures

Not all cultural and social meanings expressed through messaging money are compatible with the technological infrastructure. On April 19, 2017, WeChat Official Account announced regretfully that the Tipping function for WeChat iOS users will be shut down (wx-pai, 2017). Tipping is a functionality that often appeared at the bottom of the original content, which is published along with sections displaying the number of likes, retweets and comments. Tipping also appears on the designer's page in WeChat sticker stores (for the Chinese version of WeChat) (Figure 2.7).[4] Through Tipping, users can transfer a small amount of money of their choice (between 5 and 200 RMB) to content creators or sticker artists. This function is designed as a gifting and enjoyable gesture for users to express their appreciation, analogous to the expressive connotation of pressing the Like button on Facebook. About 11% of WeChat users had used Tipping and a great majority of them (71%) spent less than 10 RMB per month in rewarding the authors they like (China

Figure 2.7. Tip Function for Content Authors and Stickers Designers.

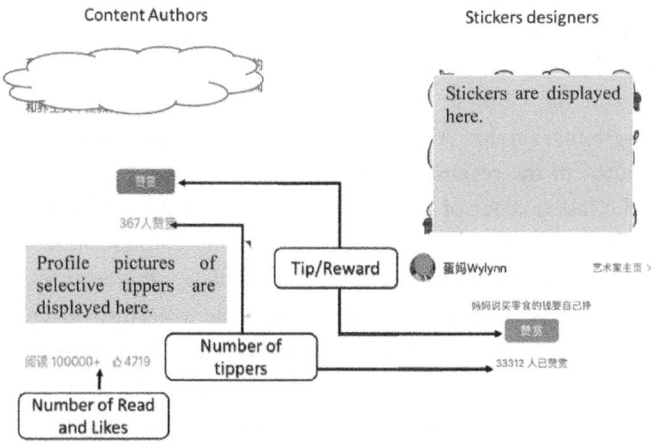

Academy of Information and Communications Technology, 2017, p. 32). The transaction is usually completed by scanning the QR codes provided by content creators or sticker designers (Figure 2.7).

WeChat had to disable this gifting function for iOS users because Apple's App Store forbids app developers from placing 'buttons, external links or other calls to action that direct customers to purchasing mechanisms other than in-app purchase' (App Store, 2016). In other words, Apple defines monetary transaction within apps such as virtual items purchase in games as purchasing behaviour which can only be allowed through Apple's own in-app purchase mechanism (IAP). Since Apple charges 30% of every transaction made through IAP and WeChat's tipping system is free of charge, Apple found WeChat Tipping violate its IAP rule. If WeChat kept the functionality, Apple would ban WeChat from App Store. In the announcement, WeChat stressed that users in other operating systems like Android had nothing to worry about.

WeChat's announcement attracted various reactions from reporters, commentators and critics, content creators and WeChat itself. Foreign newspapers voiced concerns over Apple's competition against Tencent and by extension its position in the Chinese market (Li, 2017a). China is the third largest market for Apple and in particular the leading contributor to the revenues generated from Apple's App Store – in the last quarter of 2016, Chinese users paid $ 2 billion for in-app purchases (Li, 2017b). While some Chinese industry observers and critics acknowledged Apple's adherence to its rules, others interpreted Apple's move as a gesture to curb the explosive growth of mobile payment in China (http://bit.ly/2G1dI2A). WeChat Pay and Alipay account for a combined market share of 92% in the country, where the role of Apple is minuscule (Knowledge@Wharton, 2017).

In January 2018 at a developers' conference organised by WeChat, Xiaolong Zhang, the father of WeChat, announced the return of Tipping to WeChat in the near future without disclosing any details on what changes WeChat or Apple has made or will have to make, to bring the Tipping function back. There is no evidence that the removal of Tipping had financial implications for content creators. The dispute between WeChat and Apple offers a peephole to view the infrastructural shifts for everyday payment transactions. In China, bank accounts and debit cards are more common than credit cards. WeChat Wallet along with other third-party payment platforms like Alipay represent a new type of money that minimises the effect of the preexisting payment infrastructure and the cost and investment in adopting the new technology. Hence, restaurant owners in rural areas are more likely to accept WeChat payments than credit cards issued by major banks.

Among others, what WeChat Wallet has catalysed is the infrastructural and contextual change for money transactions. Banknotes and coins embody money in circulation. Anthropologists, sociologies and media theorists have disputed economists' characterisation of money as abstract and neutral economic measurement of value by stressing that money is essentially a medium that mediates varying social relationships and symbolic meaning (Zelizer, 1997). 'Money is a social relation' (Ingham, 1996). The ability to facilitate a transaction via a smartphone transformed the infrastructure for the flow of money. 'Infrastructures of payment are hidden' (Maurer, 2015, p. 41) because usually when a business transaction takes place, sellers and buyers are more concerned about the successful flow of money to its destinations than the technological set-up to make that flow possible and successful. Infrastructure has the ability to sink into and expand from the basic or more familiar existing infrastructures

(Star & Ruhleder, 1996). It is very easy and familiar for small business owners to print something on a piece of paper. Printing out and sticking their WeChat QR code onto the wall allows small business owners to receive payments more efficiently, simplifying the set-ups for different payment terminals. This is a fundamental departure from the payment infrastructure upon which Apple's iOS operates because the latter remains card-based, but the former does not.

More importantly, WeChat boils transactions down into either scanning or messaging, or both – the same simple two-step actions that users use to add a contact, make a friend or subscribe to an Official Account on WeChat (Figure 2.5), which further hides the infrastructure of payment. Brunton (forthcoming) uses 'making money conversational' to capture the mundane ways of sending money to each other in a message box through WeChat Wallet. Texting money via mobile phones is anything but a new concept or practice, considering the popularity of M-Pesa – a widespread African service that allows people to transfer money via text messages.

Regarding WeChat Pay and mobile payment in China in general, one must note, however, that Red Packet enriches a cultural tradition but does not replace it. Placing money into a physical red envelope and handing it over to the recipient remains the most dominant ritual and most respectful expression of blessings for significant life-event celebrations such as weddings, funerals, birthdays and so on.

Secondly, e-commerce and transactions through internet-based third-party payment methods had long entered Chinese consumers' everyday life before WeChat Pay. WeChat Pay is not the first mobile payment function introduced by Tencent, either. It operates on the same legal licence for third-party payment platform that is owned by Tenpay, and Tenpay was initially developed by Tencent in 2005 to promote e-commerce on the ecosystem of QQ in programs like QQ Group Buy and QQ Hotels. Prior to WeChat Pay, the third-party payment market was dominated by Alipay – a product of Alibaba that was popularised by the boom of online shopping sites like Taobao and Tmall. Statistics show that by 2012, 80% of the internet users made a purchase through Alipay while 20% of them used Tenpay (China Internet Network Information Center, 2012). Putting aside the technical differences between Alipay and WeChat Pay, existing practices of using non-bank institutions like internet-based payment methods to facilitate everyday purchases and online consumptions are conducive to the overall boom of mobile payments in China.

The difference is that, while Alipay is often used for the purchase of more expensive items and more formal transactions such as loans, WeChat Wallet is usually the method of choice for mundane activities such as paying for breakfasts, tipping and informal group activities such as 'scrambling for red money'. In other words, unlike Alipay, WeChat Pay recreates the interfacing experience of money transaction and social interactions by bringing to core the socials aspect of money use. Messaging Red Packet (lucky, playful, or grateful money) and scan-to-pay (purchases or donations), all through and on WeChat, expresses varying social relationship involved in each specific type of money used more than simple payments.

This section demonstrates how WeChat exploits and builds on the existing cultural practices of technological use in designing its platform, which in turn reshapes social and cultural behaviours around interpersonal communication, work, socialisation, information-gathering and money use. This trajectory continues in WeChat's latest development: Mini-programs.

Mini-program, introduced in February 2017, was a service that opens up programmable access to developers (including small business/e-commerce operators and content creators) to run their lite-version apps on WeChat. If Official Accounts breaks the ground for WeChat to appify services and communication for third-parties and WeChat Pay let money circulate in the platform so that users do not have to leave the platform to get media content and services, Mini-programs opens the window for WeChat to become an app-within-app super-sticky platform. 'Mini-program is the expressive language for anything and everything,' WeChat founder Xiaolong Zhang boasted (2018). At present, WeChat is home to an estimated plethora of 580,000 apps (Ye, 2018). However, it is still too early to evaluate the impact of Mini-programs except that it fits the longer trajectory of design on WeChat – that is to mediatize and stick varying aspects of social and cultural activities together on this ever-growing mega-platform.

2.5. CONCLUSION: TECHNOLOGICAL DISRUPTION IS NOT THE RIGHT QUESTION

Has WeChat accomplished what Pony Ma envisioned of QQ at the dawn of the twenty-first century – to become the utilities of the internet? It seems that Xiaolong Zhang (2018) echoed Ma's vision when he announced in 2018 that '[Essentially] WeChat is a tool. Our goal is to build the best tool on the Internet.' WeChat is the closest a private entity has gone to become part of the digital infrastructure of Chinese society.

Chapters 1 and 2 demonstrate that technological innovations on QQ and then WeChat and popular social and cultural practices tied to mobile phones always cross-fertilise each other. A super-sticky WeChat owes as much to

Tencent's deliberate design decisions as to China's sociocultural conditions. WeChat does more to embed itself in people's everyday habits than disrupt them. This does not mean that WeChat is not transformative. On the contrary, the disappearance of technology in the eyes of WeChat users – who have to depend on WeChat for so many things – is precisely where the infrastructural power of technology lies. We tend to forget how indispensable electricity is for our daily life until the moment of the blackout. As Vincent Mosco wrote, 'It is when technologies such as the telephone and the computer cease to be sublime icons of mythology and enter the prosaic world of banality – when they lose their roles as sources of utopian visions – that they become important forces of social and economic changes' (2005, p. 6). Wendy Chun (2016) similarly argued that the power of new media is not so much concerned with its *newness* but in its embeddedness into users' habitual lives. Jay in Introduction speaks to how entrenched and mundane WeChat is in his urban life in Shanghai.

Technologies sinking into everyday cultures enrich and transform the latter, as shown most remarkably through the examples of Moments and WeChat Wallet. WeChat also widens the access to public and social services for Chinese citizens, while the platform and the holding company Tencent have never shied away from collaborating with the Chinese government. However, explorations into WeChat ought not to stop at the level of design and what users *can* do with these designs. Media scholar Tarleton Gillespie (2017) cautioned against the limitation of the platform metaphor to flatten the otherwise diverse experiences and motivations of social media users. Chapter 3 will discuss how the diverse perceptions and uses of WeChat play out in different media events.

NOTES

1. The Chinese name for Moments is pengyou quan – literarily meaning friends' circle.

2. Lucky money is also used on other celebratory occasions like birthdays and weddings.

3. Tencent is among Didi's dozen or so investors.

4. The American version of WeChat does not have Tipping function on the stickers designer's homepage.

CHAPTER 3

THE EVENTFUL WECHAT

WeChat is used for many things in everyday life. But given the political reality of contemporary China, it is not designed as a platform for social movements. Instead, it became one in practice. This chapter focuses on three instances of WeChat-facilitated social events which happened regardless of internet censorship. We shall explore how these events took place, what were their consequences and how they emerged from user practices that were based on, yet also constrained by, the mega-platform. These events include a minority group protest, exposure of a commercial scandal, and a rare scene in the Chinese literary landscape. They cut across different social groups and classes. Not as frequently, but still in a very promising manner, the participants in these events either create collective memories for participants or spur discussions on social change. When WeChat users become participants in 'WeProtest', forms of civil society emerge and challenge – albeit with limitations of political control – existing power dynamics in and outside China. The participants feel that they are involved in a larger, social process and they can make a difference. This, in turn, 'sticks' users to the mega-platform.

3.1. SOCIAL EVENTS ON CHINESE SOCIAL MEDIA

For long-time observers of China, it's no surprise that the major social incidents – those media events (Dayan & Katz, 1992) that are increasingly mediated online – matter to the general public and political regime in this authoritarian country. At certain critical moments, Chinese internet users actively participate in various movements such as nationalistic events, rights-based struggles, protests for privacy and morality, and protests against corruption (Qiu & Chan, 2009). The netizens have created collective memories of various social movements, and hence brought about institutional changes through online protest. Scholars kept a keen eye on those eventful platforms, including but not limited to Sina Weibo (Huang & Sun, 2014; Liu, 2015; Tong & Zuo, 2014), Tencent QQ (Huang & Yip, 2012), blogs (Hassid, 2012) and online forums like Baidu Tieba (Chan & Hui, 2014). They wondered to what extent the internet could reshape Chinese society and, thus, lead to liberalisation in politics. The milestones of Chinese media events include the 2008 protest against PX chemical production projects in Xiamen (Xiao, 2011; Zhou, 2011) and 2009 rallies against Maglev extension projects in Shanghai (Huang & Yip, 2012). Both these events are examples of large-scale, online-to-offline activism that was organised, promoted and facilitated by multiple internet platforms and short messaging services (SMS; Qiu, 2008; Yang, 2011b), forcing the government to compromise.

At that time, observers celebrated the role of the internet, regarding new platforms as public spheres that promised a more democratic future (Yang, 2011b). Such optimistic assumptions, however, suffered a blow when the Chinese government severely tightened up cyber censorship. The government's long observation period ended after the Arab Spring (a series of political demonstrations across the Middle East and North Africa), since which time it has become rare for officials to make compromises under the pressure of online public opinion. Shocked by social media activism, the authorities reached the conclusion that the internet poses a real threat to the regime if it's not held at bay. The government then upgraded their censorship technologies and launched cybersecurity laws, forcing platform operators to comply. Operators have to make a choice in response to the government's cyber control. Google, for example, responded by withdrawing from the Chinese search engine market, while most local platforms such as Sina Weibo agreed to the government's terms for survival. With numerous accounts and microblogs being censored on Weibo, those once-influential opinion leaders (a.k.a. Big V's) could no longer summon enough support against social injustice. In other words, they have been neutralised (Creemers, 2017).

WeChat is no exception to this general trend of heightened censorship. Indeed, the mega-platform did not hesitate to respond to the government's call for surveillance in exchange for official support. As discussed in Introduction, discourse on WeChat is managed through various censorship policies, including keyword filtering, URL blocking and Official Account supervision (Ruan et al., 2016). The *New York Times* (2016) posted a news video (http://nyti.ms/2aIZ0tm), warning that the stickiness of WeChat – those all-in-one functions that the platform provides – will make it an ideal one-stop surveillance site for Big Brother. The surveillance and control mechanism has extended to WeChat users living overseas. Under this circumstance, Wang (2016) found that the use of social media like WeChat and QQ does not necessarily translate into political empowerment. Instead, for the young migrant workers in Wang's study, 'use [of social media] tends to diminish any motivation for turning discontented thoughts into active political action' (p. 5). The asymmetrical informational power between citizens and the state, Wang continued, may help the latter 'monitor and channel public opinion (*yulun daoxiang*) and further legitimise the Chinese party-state' (ibid.).

3.2. SUPPLEMENTING, EXTENDING AND INITIATING: SOCIAL EVENTS ON WECHAT

But is this the whole picture of WeChat? Is WeChat nothing more than a palace of entertaining or a digital panopticon controlled by the government? Harwit (2016), for example, acknowledges the use of WeChat 'mainly for personal use or entertainment' (p. 6), but he further points out that the technology 'also offers Chinese citizens the potential opportunity to organise and coordinate close-knit group activities that could address issues of great community concern' (p. 6). The 'potential' that Harwit mentioned may originate either from platform design, as discussed in Chapters 1 and 2, or from the actual ways in which users deploy WeChat, including ways to re-purpose the platform for sociopolitical expressions and mobilisation. Scholars studying social movement in the contemporary world have recognised that personal connections, private networks and personalised communications play a significant part in the spread and organisation of today's collective action (Bennett & Segerberg, 2012; Papacharissi, 2010). What's special about WeChat is that it seems to combine the communication and organisational needs onto a single platform. It is, at its core, a social media platform based upon personal connections, consisting of both private (e.g., instant messaging and WeChat groups) and public channels (e.g., WeChat Moment) for users to personalise their involvement through different online actions. Those WeChat add-ons are certainly not designed for the purpose of activism, but they unintentionally nourish users' social movement practices under certain circumstances.

In this chapter, we present three roles that WeChat plays at times of major social events: the supplement, the extender and the initiator. The *supplement* role means that WeChat is used as a supplementary platform or tool, facilitating multi-platform engagement with other platforms or outlets. This usually happens in events that are less sensitive and attract less censorship. In some cases, the targets of activism are overseas entities, who are either irrelevant to the Chinese government or ideological opponents of the regime. The government is, therefore, happy to be an onlooker, if not encouraging the nationalistic expressions and mobilisation. WeChat tends to be replaceable in those events, but the overall global impact is clear: the mega-platform evokes ethnic identity among the Chinese diaspora, now present in all continents of the world.

Besides those less-sensitive cases, it's undeniable that many other media events attracted high-level censorship, either because the case challenges Big Brother's authority or goes against the interests of capitalism. Under these circumstances, when voices on other platforms are silenced or distorted, WeChat may extend online public participation, enabling users to continue discussing the topics at stake. Those discussions may not lead to institutional change in the moment, but they nevertheless create collective memories that challenge the dominant discourse of the rich and the powerful.

In other contexts, WeChat itself becomes the initial and major platform used to sustain key social events, which usually originate from WeChat Official Accounts (*weixin gonghao*) that are similar to Facebook corporate pages. User participation in and censorship of the key events take place primarily on WeChat when the involvement of other platforms becomes secondary and supplementary.

To illustrate these roles and how user practices shape WeChat-facilitated social movements from the bottom up, we choose three important events for in-depth discussion. At the centre of these three events are two males and one female, namely: Peter Liang (a NYPD policeman who is ethnic Chinese), Wei Zeixi (a college student and cancer patient who died due to incorrect medical information online) and Fan Yusu (a nanny who turned herself into a literary celebrity).

3.3. WECHAT AS SUPPLEMENT: PETER LIANG AND ONLINE ACTIVISM AMONG CHINESE AMERICANS

On 11 February 2016, a young man in the US was charged with second-degree manslaughter and sentenced to 15 years in prison. Hearing the verdict, he desperately buried his head in his hands, and his mother burst into tears. He is Peter Liang, a rookie police officer of NYPD, who was born in Hong Kong but now holds US citizenship. On 20 November 2014, Liang was on patrol in Brooklyn when his gun accidentally went off in a pitch-dark stairwell and killed an African American named Akai Gurley. This is not the first case involving US police fatally shooting innocent Black citizens, but for many Chinese Americans the legal consequences for Liang seemed to be quite different: White police officers who, also in 2014, killed Black citizens Michael Brown in Ferguson, Missouri and Eric Garner in New York faced no indictment or criminal charges, let alone conviction.

The story might have ended with Liang's imprisonment and his mother's tears, but some disputed the case as unjust. According to news coverage at the time, over 100,000 people took action by signing a petition on We the People, the White

House website, petitioning against the verdict, and through scattered protest posts and microblogs on Facebook and Twitter. What remained to be reported was the intensive mediation of the events on WeChat. Most Americans, including journalists, had not heard about this Chinese platform at that point. But hundreds of WeChat Official Accounts, mostly owned by Chinese American civic groups in US cities, posted about Liang's case right after the conviction. These articles were soon circulated by the angry and disappointed Chinese Americans in their WeChat Moment. There, a debate immediately started: is the conviction fair or racist? Some commentators and fellow Asian Americans cried out: 'Why only Liang?', 'wrong injustice'! Their anger did little to address systematic racial discriminations and police violence against African Americans (Cheng, 2016). The consensus was hard to reach, but many used their replies and likes to protest against the verdict, believing Liang was picked out for selective prosecution in the midst of Black Lives Matter. Liang was seen as a scapegoat to appease the public outcry over the police killing of Black people.

When the first debate about justice subsided, there came a second: how should the Chinese American community respond to such injustice and racism? Chinese Americans and Asian Americans in general are often stereotyped as being modest and as *not* speaking up against discrimination, let alone marching in the streets to protest injustice. The last time when Asian Americans organised themselves and took to the streets on a massive scale was in the aftermath of the Rodney King beating in 1992. This time, the WeChat users in the US decided to make some noise. A WeChat user named Huashao replied to an Official Account post about Liang by saying, 'Well, the most appropriate way (in respond to such situation) is to change the New Year Parade (i.e., tradition in many US cities that celebrates Chinese Lunar New Year) into street protests (for Liang).'

Huashao's suggestion fell upon receptive ears of the Chinese American community at large and a few civil rights Non-governmental organisations (NGOs) in particular. In addition to using public channels such as Twitter, these activist organisations also used numerous WeChat Groups that are semi-private to discuss and coordinate street protests (See Figure 3.1). Some of the groups were based in specific cities

Figure 3.1. A screenshot of WeChat Groups and Official Accounts Posts by Chinese American Communities in Various US Cities in Support of Peter Liang.

for local participants to easily identify and join. Others were national, only intended for highly influential opinion leaders and for broad mobilisation. People deliberated intensely in these WeChat Groups, asking detailed questions:

> *'How should we dress on the day of protests? And what slogans shall we use?'*
>
> *'How to avoid the conflicts between Asians and Blacks?'*
>
> *'How can we help Liang and his family?'*
>
> *'How should we promote the protest in US media? What hashtags shall we use?'*

Protest organisers received questions from WeChat Groups, discussed them and when they reached a consensus, they spread the lists of dos and don'ts to different WeChat Groups. WeChat users then further circulated the list to their Official Account and Moment, and Twitter and Facebook as well. On 20 February 2016, online activism moved offline. Tens of thousands of people rallied in 30 US cities (http://bit.ly/2FpCr0w), protesting the conviction of Liang. Those who participated in the earlier WeChat Group discussions were not surprised by how carefully the protests were organised. For example, one popular banner used by the protestors, 'One Tragedy, Two Victims,' was a response to the concern of 'Asian versus Black' addressed in WeChat discussions.

Journalists who interviewed the protestors sensed something unusual. It is of course not new that digital media mattered to social protests. What surprised the journalists was that the protestors kept mentioning the Chinese platform WeChat, alongside the well-known Twitter and Facebook, as the fertile soil for the rallies (http://lat.ms/2FiB54e). Another group who were surprised came from within the Chinese

American community – the younger generation who are supposed to be more involved in American culture. A Stanford graduate named Alice Fang, a daughter of Chinese immigrants shared her confusion and curiosity over the globalisation of WeChat and the online activism concerning Liang in her article (http://bit.ly/2Fey1KD). Fang (2016) said: 'I can't help imagining if this response (people's reactions to Liang's conviction) would have been as far-reaching if WeChat didn't exist [...] But what about WeChat has empowered this Chinese-American community in a way that, say, something like Facebook or Twitter couldn't?'

To explore this question, Fang cited her parents' WeChat experiences as examples. Fang's parents are among 50 million senior-aged (55–70 years old) WeChat users globally. Standing side by side with the middle-aged Chinese Americans, these elderly people were the backbone of this protest. According to Fang, her parents began to use WeChat not because they wanted to connect with the younger generation – who are more tech-savvy and trendy in using social media apps – but because they wanted to reconnect with their friends and relatives. This is what they could not do with Facebook and Twitter. After starting to use WeChat, Fang's parents also participated in group-buying together with their friends. Indeed, it is the older generation who were early adopters and introduced WeChat to young Chinese Americans, not the other way around. It is counterintuitive because the older generation is usually regarded as 'laggards' in adopting innovative technology (Rodgers, 1995), but now they have beaten the odds.

Fang's observation sheds light on why the Chinese American community chose WeChat, rather than more US-centric social networking sites (SNS). In the eyes of the older generation, such as Fang's parents, Twitter and Facebook are strangers' social media. WeChat is more appealing because it is in Chinese and used by their old friends and relatives back in China. Especially when communicating activities related to racism and ethnic identity, the older generation of Chinese Americans turn to the Chinese platform and discuss issues with their old pals. A platform once used for chitchat and group-buying, therefore, became a political space for mobilisation and protest. This is not to say that other SNS sites are not important. The popular hashtags like #freePeterLiang and #justice4Liang on Facebook and Twitter have demonstrated that the action supporting Peter Liang took on multiple platforms. What makes this case unique is that while the protestors used Facebook and Twitter for advocacy and explaining the protests to others, they used WeChat to mobilise and organise among themselves.

The protests in support of Peter Liang offered a peephole view of the inroads made by WeChat into the overseas Chinese community. The communication and socialisation needs among the Chinese diaspora to connect and reconnect with their homeland, relatives and friends often go unnoticed when the media spotlight is geared toward the high-profile global expansion of WeChat Pay or the skyrocketing stock price of Tencent. Communication technologies have always played a role in constructing diaspora identities. For example, anthropologist Arjun Appadurai (1996) wrote about how mass media (e.g., satellite TV) enabled immigrants to identify with their hometowns regardless of the geographical distance. Compared with mass media, online platforms like WeChat are more about personal and social connections and the more personalised ways through which WeChat 'sticks' the diasporic community to its mega-platform.

Though it is interesting to see how a platform from Asia is flowing to the West, to what extent WeChat could be globalised remained unknown. In the WeChat activism supporting Liang, there was minimal censorship from Beijing.

The Chinese government turned a blind eye to the dissemination of social movement information as long as the movement was not intended to threaten Chinese authorities (King, Pan, & Roberts, 2013). A search for relevant articles published by WeChat Official Accounts on NewRank (http://bit.ly/2tjmiEW), a third-party service provider specialising in Chinese social media content and data aggregation, generates about 500 Official Accounts that wrote about Peter Liang both before and after the protest. These Official Accounts' content either showed direct support, asking Chinese Americans to protest in the street, or celebrated the achievement of the large-scale demonstration. On April 19, 2016, nearly two months after the protests, Liang's appeal ended successfully: he was ordered to serve 5 years' probation and 800 hours of community service, but he would not spend time behind bars (http://lat.ms/20UTdG4). Meanwhile, very few of the WeChat posts were censored. Although some of the most circulated messages were later deleted, these happened possibly due to self-censorship rather than on orders from Beijing.

3.4. WECHAT THE EXTENDER: WEI ZEXI AND THE AFTERMATH OF A DEATHLY SCANDAL

'Baidu, [I] had no idea how evil it can be. Bidding rank for medical information.' (http://bit.ly/2I6gwcU) In 2016, a post on Zhihu, a peer-to-peer Q&A website similar to Quora, caught media attention in China. In reply to the question, 'What do you think is the greatest evil in human nature' (http://bit.ly/2FWxSsc), Wei Zexi, then a college student in Xi'an, wrote about his illness and experience of seeking medical information by searching on the Chinese internet giant Baidu. In 2014, Wei was diagnosed with synovial sarcoma, a rare form of cancer that threatened his young life. Doctors from different hospitals claimed that the chance of his recovery was extremely slim, but Wei and his parents did not give up. They turned to the search engine Baidu for more information on treatments. On top of the search results, they found that the Second Hospital of the Beijing Armed Police could provide cancer treatment for patients like Wei. Back then they did not know that the search results were not based on the relevance to their query. Even worse, the information about the hospital and the cancer treatment was not verified, either. It was a paid advertisement by the hospital, but Baidu did not distinguish the sponsored link from other search results. When Wei's family consulted the doctor at that hospital, they were told that the hospital's treatment had a very good recovery rate and it was 'in cooperation with Stanford University.' All these statements turned out to be a scam. Wei's family almost exhausted their savings in the hospital, but the result was devastating. On April 12, 2016, Wei died at the age of 21.

Wei's Zhihu post generated more than 60,000 responses and more than 10,000 comments. His death triggered a media campaign against Baidu's paid ranking practice as well as an exposure of a scandalous medical outsourcing industry that involved a network of private healthcare providers and many other hospitals, including the one that treated Wei. The Second Hospital of the Beijing Armed Police, a Tier-1 hospital in China, outsourced part of its services to a Shanghai-based private hospital, which belonged to the so-called 'Putian medical group', a network of more than 500 healthcare companies (Lau, 2016). These private hospitals not only operate independently but also provide treatment services to about 80 military hospitals all over the country. The Putian medical group dominates China's secondary and unregulated private healthcare market. Many of its practitioners, however, lack formal medical training and they charge an exorbitant price for substandard treatment which sometimes is clinically unapproved or even illegal (Jourdan, 2016).

From April, Chinese internet users on different digital platforms, including BBS-style Baidu Tieba, WeChat and Weibo, began to disseminate Wei's tragic story. Lawyers and doctors soon joined the online public discussion. Some officials also forwarded posts or commented on the loss of a young life. #WeiZexiBaiduPromotionIncident# became a trending hashtag on Sina Weibo that was read more than a billion times and generated hundreds of thousands of comments (Cheng, 2016). Mainstream media outlets, including the official Xinhua News Agency and the *People's Daily*, soon followed up on social media with regard to this scandal.

Initially, most media from digital platforms to mass media outlets supported Wei and accused Baidu of misleading the audience and unethically handling paid ads placements from the Putian medical group. They also questioned the quality and credibility of the Second Hospital of the Beijing Armed Police and by extension the regulatory loopholes in the military hospital system. Local media reported that the government had stepped in to investigate both the hospital and Baidu's online search business (http://bit.ly/2HbyNVb). At this stage, the censorship machine targeted those who pointed their fingers at the Armed Police, but not others. Chinese Armed Police is a paramilitary force to safeguard domestic security (e.g., anti-terrorism, disaster relief). It differs from the regular police force due to its military background and leadership (Guo, 2012). In China, the military is the backbone of communist rule. Criticising the military thus crosses the red line of censorship.

As the discussion about Wei's death continued online, different voices surfaced, which may raise a few eyebrows. One year after his death, Wei's Baidu Tieba forum (retrieved on July 2017) carried posts that defended Baidu or blamed Wei. For instance, some started a discussion thread with titles like 'Don't blame Baidu' (http://bit.ly/2I5pozF) and 'I still don't understand why it has to do with Baidu.' (http://bit.ly/2Fvs0IQ). Others blamed Wei and questioned his common sense knowledge by asking: 'Wei is a college student, [so] shouldn't he know better?' (http://bit.ly/2H83ri1) Except for those who self-identified as Baidu employees, we do not know if these pro-Baidu posts represent an online public opinion. Similar posts also appeared on Zhihu, which eventually blocked six accounts with over 621,000 followers in total. According to Zhihu (2016), these account holders 'colluded for inappropriate exposure' and 'violated Zhihu's regulations.' But some internet users were not convinced. They suspected that the blocked users had been 'bought' by Baidu to whitewash the incident (http://bit.ly/2I92He4).

The revelation of Baidu's problematic bidding rank practice and the Putian medical group was a joint effort by many internet users who used all kinds of media technologies including WeChat. Specifically, according to NewRank, there were 13,754 WeChat accounts with 26,525 posts about Wei's tragedy, attracting 135 million clicks and 1.3 million likes. People enthusiastically circulated these messages in their WeChat Moment, and 243 of these posts received more than 100,000 clicks each. On April 30, there were only six posts; however, the number of posts and articles soared to 278 on May 1 and reached its peak of 5,403 on May 3. Initially, the most-read posts fiercely criticised Baidu and the sub-standard hospitals. For example, in a widely circulated article published on WeChat entitled 'Why Baidu is the greatest evil (see attached list of Putian hospitals),' (http://bit.ly/2H9IMKL) the author called Wei Zexi 'a young man who died at the hands of Baidu and a military hospital.' Posts that fiercely attacked Baidu were not censored on WeChat, not so much because of the nature of the event, but probably because WeChat's parent company Tencent is a direct competitor against Baidu in the internet business.

But WeChat also played a subtle and sustaining role during Wei's tragedy before the scandal broke. Scholars have long acknowledged the power of online platforms such as Sina Weibo and public forums in boosting the online public sphere and popularising citizen activism in China (Yang, 2011b). Studies also showed that patients with specific diseases used social media to form online communities to share experiences, exchange clinical information and give or receive emotional support (Greene, Choudhry, Kilabuk, & Shrank, 2011). In Wei's story, WeChat seemed to have also created a more intimate and supportive space which other platforms had failed to provide. Mainly communicating in a WeChat private group, Wei and his family and friends found support, financially and emotionally, and others personalised their micro-philanthropic activities and expressions of compassion.

Wei's first attempt to seek the public's help took place on Sina Weibo, according to his friend who wrote a remembrance post by using Wei's Weibo account after his death. The friend explained, 'When Wei Zexi was still alive, he could not afford the medical treatment. The reason to open this Weibo account was to get media attention, but there were few responses [...]' (http://bit.ly/2tnhWwi)

Given the cold shoulder on Weibo, a WeChat Group became the place of action before Wei's case blew up as a media event. More than 250 people joined a WeChat Group named 'Helping Zexi' (http://bit.ly/2D3iDdU) after reading his story on Zhihu and other platforms. Others who did not join the group added Wei and his parents as friends on WeChat and communicated with them directly. In either private group discussions or direct conversations with Wei and his family, they discussed Wei's plight and provided tremendous support. In Wei's initial post exposing Baidu's evilness, he shared some screenshots from WeChat discussions and said that he was 'very moved' by his WeChat friends for buying him medicines from Hong Kong (http://bit.ly/2I6gwcU). Some of those who knew about Wei from Zhihu and Weibo — two public platforms — bonded with Wei and his families and friends by moving into a relatively more private space created by WeChat (Figure 3.2).

Specifically, WeChat helped extend Wei's story in two ways. First, it provided an alternative space for discussions about Baidu's questionable search results and later whitewashing attempts. In a different event, WeChat played a similar role to sustain public discussions when censorship was enacted effectively on other media platforms. Around the Chinese New Year of 2015, a famous journalist named Chai Jing released her documentary online about air pollution in China, 'Under the Dome.' (http://bit.ly/17JY1HV) The public responded enthusiastically, but the authorities soon intervened to clamp down on online discussion, prohibiting reports on the documentary. The documentary was then

Figure 3.2. WeChat Screenshot Posted by Wei Zexi on Zhihu.

banned. Relevant videos and discussions were removed. However, discussions continued in peer-to-peer messaging and in-group chat on WeChat. The setting of WeChat Moment allowed users to select the audience for their posts, which granted users certain degree of security to share opinions online (Wang & Gu, 2016)

Secondly, WeChat directed public attention to a more private space. Directly reporting and publicising their situation in the private WeChat Group and through Wei's own Moments, Wei and his family engaged their supporters in a more intimate and personal manner, and vice versa. Wei's supporters could also transfer money through WeChat Wallet directly to Wei. WeChat helped effectively transforming onlookers into active supporters. Without WeChat and its stickiness that sustained Wei's first appeal for help, Wei's death and the subsequent exposure of Baidu's scandalous business of paid ranking and the Putian medical group would never have become such a major social event. Private engagements and personalised micro-donations could easily go off our radar, but they are critical for sustaining the struggle while being less likely to be censored.

3.5. WECHAT THE INITIATOR: WHO IS FAN YUSU, AND WHY DO PEOPLE CARE?

'My life is a book that is clumsily bound by destiny, which makes it unbearable for people to read.' This lead sentence opens an autobiography entitled 'I Am Fan Yusu,' published by the WeChat Official Account, Zhengwu, on April 24, 2017. In the nearly 8,000-word autobiographic essay, Fan, a nanny and migrant worker living in Beijing, talked about her mother's love, the family's life in rural China, her life as a single mother running away from an abusive husband and then migrating to the big city, her jobs as a nanny and then also as a teacher for migrant children living in Beijing's far outskirts. She also wrote about her two daughters. There was no sensational scandal in her writing. No provocative statement. No eye-catching photo. Not even a clickbait title. Taking about 20 minutes to complete, it is a relatively long read for WeChat users who do their reading on the smartphone. 'I Am Fan Yusu' seemed, on the surface, to lack important features that would make it go viral.

But it did, overnight. 'I Am Fan Yusu' received more than 100,000 clicks in a few hours after its publication via Zhengwu, which was shared through WeChat Moment as well as WeChat Groups all over the country. In 3 days, there were 750 follow-up posts about Fan Yusu published in various WeChat Official Accounts. In total, they generated over four million clicks and tens of thousands of retweets and shares. Never before had a piece of writing by an unknown migrant worker, or by anyone for that matter, received so much public attention in the history of Chinese internet. This was also a very rare scene in China's literary landscape.

Who is Fan Yusu? What is so special about her story? Fan was a 44-year-old domestic worker in Beijing. She wrote in a simple and straightforward manner, but with poetic sensitivity to portray the struggles, bitterness and unwavering persistency of a woman who lived on the margins of society but held her head up high when facing difficulties in life. From her story, we learned that her mother gave everything she had to raise her five children in the countryside; that Fan started to read literature such as *Oliver Twist* and *Robinson Crusoe* in her early teens; and that she had once been married to an alcoholic and then ran away from him with her daughters.

To survive and escape from 'boring rural life,' Fan moved to Beijing at the age of 20 and became a domestic helper working for a wealthy man's mistress. She took care of an infant girl in a mansion while leaving her elder daughter to take care of her younger daughter because she only had one day off each week. Fan (2017) wrote using dark humour about the power dynamics between men and women and between the rich and the poor:

> *Concubine's body is more beautiful and curvy than a model's. Her face is even prettier than Fan Bingbing, the movie star [...] But she has to give up her dignity and kneels down to beg for food (from my male employer). I am confused. Is it Tang Dynasty, Qing Dynasty, or socialist China I am living in? Yet I don't have supernatural powers, [so] I can't time-travel!*

Poignant and defiant, Fan's writing touches on issues of class and gender inequality, thereby challenging China's hierarchical social order, its patrimony and hypocrisy. The working class was once glorified in the newborn People's Republic of China, but now it has become a label for the poor, the less educated and those looked down upon, an abhorrent status often associated with rural-to-urban migrant workers like Fan herself. Fan's remarkable thinking and her literary skills have smashed the derogatory stereotype of the working class. More important, in becoming the voice of voiceless grassroots migrants, Fan suddenly became a modern Chinese version of Martin Eden, the working-class protagonist who educated himself into a famous literary figure in Jack London's novel of the same name.

All around the country, internet users were eager to share, via their WeChat Moment, Fan's autobiography and other reports about her. News organisations and other internet platforms soon realised that the story could attract more traffic. They competed to report on Fan, to either praise her work and talents or conduct muckraking investigations against Fan, her past, and her family. Journalists used the same words, which were accurate: 'overnight fame' (Guan, 2017; Ouyang, 2017). Fan became such a celebrity, and there were so many interview requests, that she could not carry on her normal life. So she left and reportedly hid in an ancient temple deep in the mountains – at least that was what journalists were told. She announced her decision to step away from the spotlight via a WeChat message to her friend.

But in reality, we learned from a private WeChat Group consisting of Fan Yusu's close friends and supporters that she remained in her shabby rental room, reading, writing and reflecting. This WeChat Group was based on an offline gathering called Pi Village Workers' Literary Group that came together on weekends to read, write and discuss contemporary Chinese literature in relation to working-class culture. For years, Fan took an active part in the offline meetings, while sharpening her literary senses and skills through working with fellow migrants sharing her interests and experiences. Like in the case of Wei Zexi, it took a collective effort to re-shape WeChat into a tool of major social events. The difference is that, for Fan Yusu and her comrades, the social support group first built their solidarity through physical meetings in a particular locale – Pi Village on the verge of Beijing – before they congregated online through WeChat.

The Fan Yusu phenomenon – as some would call it – entered the public realm and then exited it with a string of WeChat posts. Fan carried on with her life. Her sudden fame on social media, nonetheless, offers a glimpse into the issues around workers' digital literacy and media representations of class. With few exceptions, Chinese working-class culture has been obscured in the mass media. An outstanding example of working-class cultural activities entering the mainstream is the Migrant Workers' Spring Festival Gala starting in 2012, a show celebrating Chinese Lunar New Year, whose main organisational structure happens to be in Pi Village as well. Indeed, this is the same grassroots organisation that started and sustained the workers' literary group of which Fan is an active member. Years before Fan's 'overnight fame', the Migrant Workers' Spring Festival Gala had been broadcast live nationwide via satellite TV and online video sites despite its modest budget, allowing workers to take the stage and express themselves to a wider audience (Han, 2013; Mo, 2015). It was probably not a coincident that Fan Yusu came from Pi Village, where worker-artists had long taken initiatives such as Migrant Workers' Spring Festival Gala in order to re-shape societal perceptions of the working class.

As a migrant worker, Fan Yusu's story manifests a long struggle to reclaim the power of self-representation and storytelling by the Chinese working class. Before Fan, workers' self-presentation could rarely reach out to other social groups such as the urban middle class. Yet Fan succeeded in crossing the class boundary and appealing to a very broad audience pool beyond individual class positions. In this case, WeChat was way more than an affordable communication tool and a broadcasting platform. It also allowed Chinese people of different social status to subscribe to numerous Official Accounts based on their personal interests. In so doing, the collective user practices from the bottom up, by Fan Yusu and her comrades, in and outside Pi Village, reversed the power dynamics between mainstream media and workers' voice, between the working class and affluent urban employers.

From an activist's perspective, Fang's post was at most a very soft version of protest. Yet the extraordinary attention it received turned into something worrisome – not for censors in the Chinese government, but for self-censors within WeChat in this case. According to two sources who are familiar with WeChat's operation, managers of the mega-platform decided to remove 'I am Fan Yusu' three days after its publication. The reason was that WeChat managers believed such a high volume of traffic — four million hits in three days — would very likely trigger official censorship. Thus, they decided to strike pre-emptively before receiving the order from the authorities. In other words, WeChat could be reshaped from the bottom up by user practices as shown in 'Fan Yusu phenomenon'. But the ultimate power is still in the hands of the authorities and their corporate proxies inside the platform's operational team. If they perceive a threat, be it real or not, the structural design of WeChat means the top-down logic of censorship and/or self-censorship would still dominate. The role of WeChat in initiating major social events is, therefore, still limited.

3.6. CONCLUSION

Events are special historical moments that play a unique part in shaping people's memories and understandings about who they are, what they can achieve and where they are heading for. Events do not happen every day. But when they happen nowadays in Chinese society — including overseas Chinese communities from New York to New Zealand — chances are they would occur in part or in full on the mega-platform of WeChat. This should come as no surprise because WeChat is so 'sticky' that average Chinese social media users spend the majority of their online time on WeChat anyway, no matter whether they are old or young, male or female. When news events like Peter Liang and Fan Yusu happen, it is only natural that they use WeChat as the most convenient channel to get updates and spread the word.

But WeChat is also much more than just a place for information exchange. Its super-stickiness means it offers users multiple functions to meet their different needs in communication, mobilisation and coordination. It also serves as a central network in China's new media system connecting Weibo and Zhihu with Baidu Tieba and other online forums in the making of large-scale, impactful social events. The power of WeChat lies in its ability to initiate discussions and break old patterns of user practices. It also lies in its capacity to supplement other media channels and extend issues of public concern into the realm of collective action. As can be seen in the cases of Wei Zexi and Fan Yusu, the most crucial function is arguably WeChat Group, whose semi-private nature means participants can discuss among themselves relatively freely. These are also high-trust networks from whence collective action may emerge and scale up from sporadic practices that may, at times, re-shape the culture of the platform.

We see WeChat Group as 'semi-private' because the platform is still under the watchful eyes of Chinese internet censors, who may intervene any time they want. Although they usually choose to be more tolerant regarding socio-political discussions among overseas Chinese, a small number of sensitive words are nevertheless removed when using overseas versions of the WeChat app (Ruan et al., 2016). Within the People's Republic of China, there are much higher levels of censorship by government agencies and self-censorship by internet users, content providers and corporate players such as WeChat itself. Therefore, if we compare WeChat-facilitated social events since 2013 with their equivalents based on Weibo, the Twitter-like service that once dominated the Chinese social media landscape before 2013 (Han, 2016), the overall patterns cannot be more clear: as the frequency of 'subversive' events has declined, so has the intensity of conflicts and the number of protesters who took part in public demonstrations after using social media.

The commercial logic of the platform has been captured by the political rationale of the regime. From there, user practices are shaped, limited to the personal and interpersonal discussions that rarely lead to offline public gatherings, confined to the cultural and consumerist spheres that seldom challenge the status quo of systematic inequality. However, underneath this larger pattern of observations, we'd like to emphasise that user practices from the bottom up still matter, not only globally outside China per se but also within the country where victims of injustice, outspoken citizens, migrant workers, journalists and other types of professionals still have room to develop alliances and push for change, through WeChat or by using it as an integral part of multimodal media strategy. There is still hope despite the reality of censorship. If future events take place that fundamentally change China, then there is still a fair chance they may occur on the super-sticky platform of WeChat.

CHAPTER 4

CONCLUSION: SUPER-STICKY WECHAT AND THE GLOBAL SOCIETY

4.1. A MODERN CHINESE SOCIAL TECHNOLOGY ON EXHIBIT

In September 2017, the Victoria and Albert Museum (V&A) in London added WeChat to its Design, Architecture and Digital (DAD) collections. This decision makes V&A the first museum in the world to collect a social media application and WeChat the first contemporary Chinese social technology entering a Western museum. V&A explained the motive for the acquisition, 'As a social media platform designed to quickly respond to users' needs and lifestyles, WeChat has arguably had more impact on Chinese society than any digital design in recent history. It thus became fundamentally important for us to find a way for it to be captured at this moment in time and preserved for the future' (Cormier, 2017). A demo phone with a special version of WeChat installed is on display. It allows visitors and researchers to explore the features without connecting to the server. V&A's news release for the WeChat collection reads: 'Since its launch in 2011, WeChat has grown from a simple 'chat app' to encompass an entire mobile-centric intelligent lifestyle and aims to connect its nearly one billion users to the people, businesses, and services that they care about' (The Victoria and Albert Museum, 2017).

For a cursory visitor to V&A's WeChat collection, the demo phone may only offer a 'tech tasting' of what users can do with WeChat. Like all other museum objects, the disconnected WeChat presents a diluted experience detached from the real-world culture and society, hence leaving behind an array of media and technological practices associated with the mega-platform. Historians and researchers in the future, however, may still be able to piece together a more complete picture of what WeChat can say about social media and about Chinese culture and society in the early twenty-first century, just like how contemporary historian Thomas Mullaney (2017) deciphers what happened when typewriters first entered China in the twentieth century.

Rewind a hundred years or so, the idea of designing and manufacturing a Chinese typewriter was ridiculed and engineers found it impossible to make Chinese characters compatible with a typing technology based on alphabetic languages (Mullaney, 2017). The Chinese script was soon blamed for being unfit for and thus inferior to modernity. Mullaney (2017) presented a fascinating study on the attempts to solve the challenge posed by a Chinese typewriter and how these attempts, successful or not, revealed less about the mechanics of typewriter design than the racialised framework of technology and the cultural biases against non-Western languages. When finally equipped for mass manufacturing, the Chinese typewriters in use still somehow resembled their

Conclusion

Western counterparts. Instead of typing, as Mullaney (2017) observed, operators on a Chinese typewriter, do more work of *pre-selecting* frequently used Chinese characters and *organising* them on the tray bed, and the machines were *felt* and *experienced* differently by Chinese typists because they involved physical motions and coordination that were never associated with using a typewriter for English.

In an uncanny analogy, the Chinese typewriter and WeChat in V&A, a hundred years apart, both teach us how universality and specificity of technologies always intertwine. As media theorist Wendy Chun wrote, technological mediation is 'always already a mix of science, art, and culture' (Chun, 2011, p. 39). When the technology of typewriting landed in China, it encountered a different society from its origin. It is the language, social norms and customary practices that impacted on how Chinese typewriter came into being and was made to work. Today, quite a few web-based applications fall under the umbrella term social media. Not only individual social media platforms differ from each other, but also the same social media app is used differently across cultures (Miller et al., 2016). Hence, a look into WeChat – its design and functionalities, its business model and social impact, its trajectories of development – shall give us a better understanding of social media globally, beyond the Anglophone world.

Throughout the book, we delineate how WeChat 'quickly responds to users' needs and lifestyles' in China through the term: super-sticky. *Super-sticky* describes 1) the developmental character of WeChat whose services and functionalities expand and deepen the penetration of the mega-platform into the social fabrics of everyday life and 2) the cohesive – even adhesive – character of WeChat that not only glues a number of services together but also glues diverse users (e.g. governmental agencies and commercial players) to the platform. In a way, this is not entirely new because other internet companies like Facebook, Google and even WeChat's sibling QQ have all displayed the tendency to expand and try to absorb users of different kinds. Nonetheless, WeChat seems to have stood out from all social media platforms in the world due to its successes in implementing the rules of sticky design through its daily business operations. WeChat has achieved what most others can only dream of. In an unprecedented way, its growing number of services fulfils users' social and transactional needs, which further enhances users' dependence upon the mega-platform. In comparison, for instance, Facebook derives most of its revenue from data-driven, targeted advertising, so the services Facebook offers centre upon reaping more data from its users. From every change made to its terms of services to its new add-on services, all measures reinforce the tendency to extract more data (McKeon, 2010). WeChat of course also collects large amounts of data on its users, for its own use, for sale and for sharing with the powers that be. But this is, comparatively speaking, a much smaller and much less central part of WeChat's business revenues which also come from games, emoji sticker sales, third-party services, in-platform financial transactions and so on.

The book offers insights into WeChat's development trajectory towards a mega-platform while situating it within the Chinese context. We recognise that WeChat's technological innovations have greatly impacted users' behaviours and Tencent's business performance. The central message of the book also highlights the popular techno-social practices in China associated with mobile phones, which date from before the birth of WeChat and will probably have far-reaching implications for future technologies of all kinds, not just social media.

4.2. WECHAT-ISE EVERYDAY LIFE?

Super-sticky WeChat responds to users' needs and established ways of life in China, and in so doing it also reshapes Chinese lifestyles on its mobile interface. WeChat is a social media app in that a great majority of activities happening on it are interpersonal communication and 'creation and sharing users-generated contents' (Kaplan & Haenlein, 2010, p. 61). According to Miller and colleagues (2016, p. xxvii), sociality is scalable by the spectrum from being private to public and the size of the interactive social group. WeChat is a private-facing app designed to favour small-group interactions.

But as a techno-social creation, WeChat is much more than a platform of user-generated content. WeChat, after the integration of Wallet, assumes a strong pro-business tendency. Here WeChat is both transformative and conservative. Economic activities are an indispensable part of social interactions. Early information and communication technologies (ICT) do not tend to separate users' social interactions from economic activities. People used letters, telegraphs, telephones and computers for both business and social purposes. It was only in recent years that the term social media was popularised and used to describe a particular family of technological applications. By bringing economic activities back to the realm of technological mediation where social activities also take place, WeChat is better able to fit into everyday practices, thus continuing a long course of interactions between ICT and society in which social media platforms such as Facebook and Twitter are aberrations instead of the norm.

On the other hand, nonetheless, WeChat has done more to preserve than change the status quo of the social and political structure. Its holding company Tencent remains comfortably on the path of 'state-led, market-driven' (Zhao, 2007) digital capitalism whilst the company reaps huge profits from its business success as long as the government maintains control over content, society and the ownership of and access to a variety of ICT infrastructure, on which WeChat becomes the latest additional layer.

From its humble beginning in the 1990s until 2016, Tencent had declared that its mission is '[to] enhance people's quality of life through internet services' and that they 'aim to create values for users' (Tencent, 2016a).[1] In early 2018, its mission became:

'To enhance the quality of life through internet services:

- To treat the internet like electricity: a fundamental service that is reliable and makes life easier and more enjoyable.

- To address the diverse needs of different regions and consumers by offering differentiated products and services.

- To build a healthy, win-win internet ecosystem based on open collaboration with partners' (Tencent, 2018).

Corresponding to the increasingly strategic importance of WeChat in the company's business map, Tencent shifts away from 'creat[ing] values for users' through value-added services and toward equating itself as the utility of the internet age – an all-purpose, seemingly neutral technology.

Writing prior to the time of WeChat Pay, Eric Harwit (2017) was perceptive about the implications of WeChat for future social and political development. He wrote, 'WeChat will likely continue to develop mainly as a new technology that meets the needs of citizens who seek intimate, personal and locally oriented communication. Hence, it will foster a trend to social atomisation and thereby slow the movement toward the formation of a large digital civil society' (Harwit, 2017, p. 13). Our book demonstrates that the super-sticky model also brings WeChat and Tencent into a more intimate, if not mutually dependent, relationship with the Chinese government. Compliant technology and close ties with the authorities pave the way to glory for WeChat.

Close ties with the government, however, do not necessarily have fully negative connotations. As discussed in Chapters 2 and 3, WeChat is among other tech companies aspiring to serve the public by facilitating services (e.g. doctor's appointments, charitable donations) that used to be either absent or unevenly distributed due to a weak civil society.

4.3. GLOBAL INFLUENCE OF THE SUPER-STICKY MODEL

Jay's statement in the Introduction that 'Leaving WeChat means leaving [social] life' offers a glimpse into how embedded WeChat has become in the daily life of China. However, WeChat's limited reach beyond the Chinese-speaking world makes it tempting to conclude that WeChat is only relevant to Chinese society.

If it only flourishes in the insulated Chinese market, we ask, does WeChat matter to the entire world? Or, if only proven to be successful among Chinese users, can WeChat's super-sticky strategy still work when it expands globally? What could it suggest for the world of social media to have such a super-sticky model?

In reality, WeChat's model has already gone beyond China. Its all-inclusive design approach already has regional and global imitators. A notable example is the Vietnamese social media app Zalo, which was released in August 2012 (https://apple.co/1RuLPND). Browsing through its features, we found its appearance and featured functionalities extremely similar to WeChat. The only major difference is the theme colour – Zalo is blue. Apart from the interface, Zalo also 'copied' WeChat's all-in-one model. Both have instant message functioning as their core, and e-commerce, online media, multimedia chatting and blog-like Official Account services as their derivatives (https://bit.ly/2pLn9sP). Zalo also introduces scan QR code as a means to add new contacts, though it lacks a payment function. Zalo has won millions of users in Vietnam (https://bit.ly/2I709MG). https://bit.ly/2I709MG).

Another interesting app is YakChat, launched by the Tibetan community in exile in Dharamsala, India. According to a *Foreign Policy* article, Dharamsala is 'one of the most hacked places in the world' because it is 'ground zero in China's cyberwar' (Kaiman, 2013, p. 35). WeChat was also popular here, so popular that it was seen as a security threat. 'All of the traffic is being channelled through Shanghai,' said an interviewee in the article, 'It's presumably being piped into China's equivalent of PRISM.' Their response: 'a secure Tibetan-language messaging application called YakChat' (Kaiman, 2013, p. 36). The functions of YakChat indeed look very similar to WeChat except for its logo of a cute Tibetan yak, and the most important difference that it's owned and operated by Tibetans in Dharamsala, India.

Outside Asia, we see other developments that went parallel with or were triggered by what was going on within WeChat. WhatsApp introduced voice message in 2013. Apple opened its App Store to designers who sell animated stickers and incorporated those animated stickers into iMessage (Apple, 2016). Facebook introduced peer-to-peer money transfer on its Messenger platform (Perez, 2017), a move toward enriching services associated with messaging – until then, a distinctive feature of WeChat. Super-sticky design, in this sense, is no longer a Chinese-only characteristic of one idiosyncratic platform. It has become a trend affecting the Western world, too.

A major shift in technological innovation has taken place, as seen in the case of WeChat — and to a lesser extent, its sibling platform QQ. Namely, a developing-world app, once accused of being a 'copy-cat', now becomes a model of emulation, if not a source of inspiration, for companies in Western countries as well. To world system theorists, this reflects a new global flow of technology from China (Chase-dunn, 1997; Radice, 2009). WeChat on display at the V&A Museum — a museum owing its very foundation to the UK's colonial past — also shows that social media systems can travel in the opposite direction against the dominant flows of imperialism. Has WeChat achieved what Daya Thussu (2006) called 'contra-flow' of media products? In his *Media on the Move: Global Flow and Contra-Flow*, Thussu observed such 'countra-flow' as follows:

> *Though the Northern conglomerates continue to shape the global media landscape, the flow of global media products is not just one way from the media-rich North (and within it the Anglo-American axis) to the media-poor South. There is evidence that in an increasingly global communication environment, new transnational networks have emerged, including from the periphery to the metropolitan centres of global media. (Thussu, 2006, p. 2)*

Thussu based his argument on studies of a Latin American telenovela (Rego & La Pastina, 2006), Bollywood movies (Govil, 2006) and media experts from Japan and Korea (Iwabuchi, 2006; Kim, 2006). Media globalisation used to be regarded as Westernisation or Americanisation until the aforementioned media products started to flow from East to West, from South to North. Although Thussu made his point before social media and smartphones, the concept of contra-flow remains helpful despite a few qualifications.

Some scholars maintain that the 'metropolitan centres' of the West continue to enjoy global dominance, for instance, Google, Facebook, Twitter and Instagram (van Dijck, 2016). We can only recognise WeChat as the latest example of contra-flow if we bear in mind that the company is embedded in an authoritarian media system of censorship and surveillance. For this matter, WeChat is not going to defeat Facebook any time soon and it only has a limited impact on the global power dynamics of the worldwide social media industry. In fact, the pro-business shift in recent years is likely to further constrain WeChat's potential to disrupt existing patterns of global media flow. Compared with media products exported to the West (e.g., Bollywood movies and Japanese anime), the content and users of WeChat stay decisively Chinese. By now, WeChat's overseas reach is largely confined to the Chinese diaspora. Although its WeChat Pay, in particular, has expanded to countries like Japan, the platform's overall attraction and usage to non-Chinese speakers awaits further evidence. For this reason, in Peter Liang's case (mentioned in Chapter 3), the Chinese Americans had to deploy a multi-platform strategy, promoting their protests across WeChat, Twitter and Facebook. Otherwise, their voices could not be heard by other sectors of American society.

Seen from the perspective of market capitalisation, however, WeChat has already surpassed the global contra-flow examples that Thussu identified. By February 2018, Tencent's stock-market valuation is worth more than that of Facebook (https://bit.ly/2IXKfFE), whereas Bollywood remains far behind Hollywood in terms of its total market value https://bitly/2IXKfFE).

Nonetheless, considering Wall Street's enthusiasm in pursuing Tencent's soaring stocks, we can say that WeChat has a much stronger capacity to lure global investors than global social media users. This revelation is at once profound and ironic because the money from the supposedly liberal world supports such a super-sticky model that is also tolerated, if not encouraged, by an authoritarian government. A future permeated with surveillance technologies worries many observers (Chun, 2018; Kessel & Mozur, 2016; Wang, 2017). In their eyes, the line between an all-in-one platform and the omnipresent Big Brother is too thin to be meaningful. More important, this model can be easily adapted in liberal democracies (Kessel & Mozur, 2016). For them, WeChat and China represent the nightmare of tomorrow, the real-world renditions of *Black Mirror* that are more down-to-earth, more quotidian, more frightening and with more financial power (Chun, 2018; Kessel & Mozur, 2016; Wang, 2017).

4.4. SOCIAL MEDIA AT CROSSROADS

The ultimate irony, however, is not about WeChat as the exception or the rule. Nor is it about total surveillance and our chance to steer away. On first glance, Tencent has many of the same institutional investors who also back Facebook, Google, Amazon, Apple and other global tech giants. Like the real estate sector, the tech industry has become a favourite child of global capital, regardless of the company's nationality (Jia & Winseck, 2018; Srnicek, 2016). Yes, we ought to be concerned about the dystopian future, about the ubiquitous and super-sticky WeChat and how it serves the Chinese authorities through devices such as the new social credit system (Botsman, 2017). But the real threat is that *all* social media companies in the world are trying to neglect their social responsibilities in pursuit of profit maximisation.

Instead of exoticizing WeChat as another oriental techno-object, we ought to be attentive to what WeChat and its Western counterparts such as Facebook have in common. As of this writing in March 2018, Western media was awashed with stories of Cambridge Analytica and its mishandling of user data at Facebook for political manipulation during the 2016 US election. Mainstream media finally stumbled to catch up with what scholars have warned about for years about the debilitating political implications of surveillance capitalism (see for example, Cohen, 2008; Tufekci, 2014; Zimmer, 2010; Zuboff, 2015). The Cambridge Analytica disaster, along with Facebook's scandalous emotional experiments in 2014 and others incidents, reveal the deep structural flaws associated with the business models of tech companies being driven, regardless of their location, by the power of financial capitalism. We are already at the centre of a global storm questioning the future directions for social media platforms. How to define the liabilities for these tech companies? How to shape their policies and behaviours so that, from now on, they have no choice but to act responsibly – not only for their investors and Big Brother watching over their shoulders but also for all social media users, for the citizenry online and offline? These are the first questions we have to answer concerning any social media platform, be it Facebook or WeChat.

NOTE

1. The webpage was last accessed on December 6, 2016.

APPENDIX

A TIMELINE OF WECHAT (FROM NOVEMBER 2010 TO JANUARY 2018)

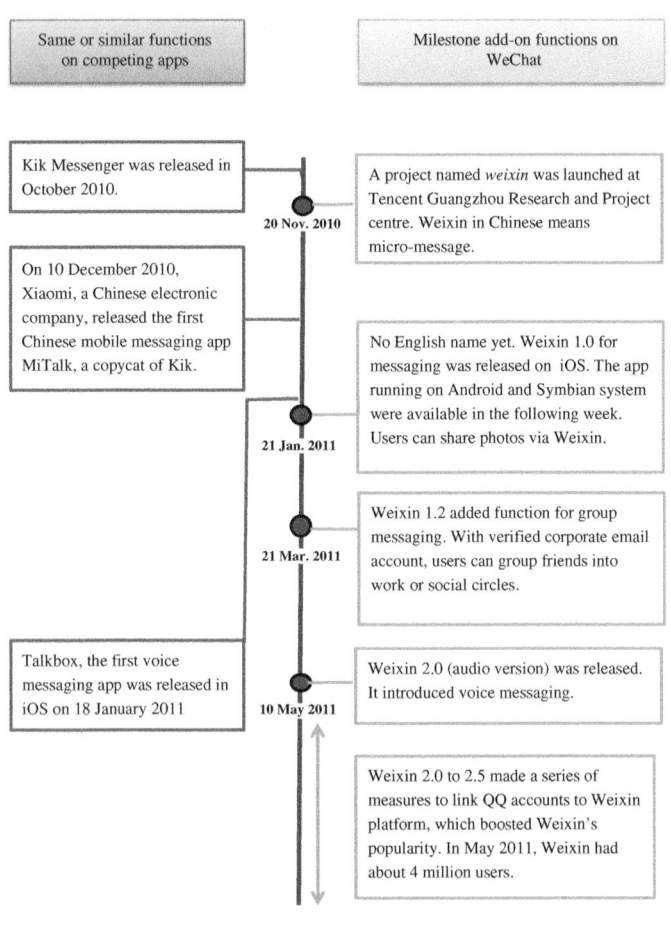

Appendix

03 Aug. 2011	Momo, a location-based hook-up app in China, was released on 3 August 2011. People Nearby is its signature.
03 Aug. 2011	Weixin 2.5 introduced video clipping and allowed users to add contacts by searching people in proximity, a function called People Nearby. Hereafter, the number of new users reached a peak of 100,000.
	In August 2011, LINE, a social networking app started in Japan, introduced the function of Shake. LINE also introduced scanning QR code service and Sticker Store.
18 Oct. 2011	Weixin 3.0 allowed users to add each other as contacts by simultaneously shaking their phones. The function was called Shake.
27 Oct. 2011	Weixin 3.1 introduced English interface. Until now Weixin was only available in traditional and simplified Chinese.
10 Dec. 2011	Weixin 3.5 allowed users to generate QR code for their account and to add new contacts by scanning QR code. It also introduced dynamic emoticons.
30 Mar. 2012	Weixin user numbers reached 100 million. That is 433 days after its initial release.
19 Apr. 2012	WeChat 4.0 added new functions: **My Posts Moments**. My Posts is a picture-oriented timeline. Users can share pictures with social updates and post comments on Moments. WeChat 4.0 also opened its API allowing third-parties to plug-in onto the platform owning their **Public Accounts**.

Appendix

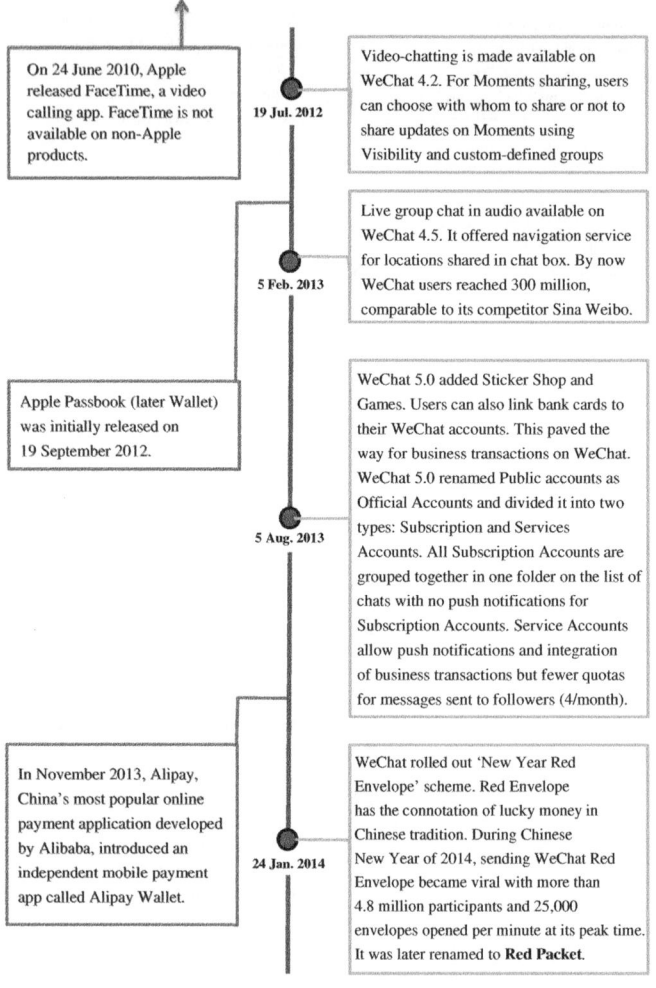

On 24 June 2010, Apple released FaceTime, a video calling app. FaceTime is not available on non-Apple products.

19 Jul. 2012 — Video-chatting is made available on WeChat 4.2. For Moments sharing, users can choose with whom to share or not to share updates on Moments using Visibility and custom-defined groups

5 Feb. 2013 — Live group chat in audio available on WeChat 4.5. It offered navigation service for locations shared in chat box. By now WeChat users reached 300 million, comparable to its competitor Sina Weibo.

Apple Passbook (later Wallet) was initially released on 19 September 2012.

5 Aug. 2013 — WeChat 5.0 added Sticker Shop and Games. Users can also link bank cards to their WeChat accounts. This paved the way for business transactions on WeChat. WeChat 5.0 renamed Public accounts as Official Accounts and divided it into two types: Subscription and Services Accounts. All Subscription Accounts are grouped together in one folder on the list of chats with no push notifications for Subscription Accounts. Service Accounts allow push notifications and integration of business transactions but fewer quotas for messages sent to followers (4/month).

In November 2013, Alipay, China's most popular online payment application developed by Alibaba, introduced an independent mobile payment app called Alipay Wallet.

24 Jan. 2014 — WeChat rolled out 'New Year Red Envelope' scheme. Red Envelope has the connotation of lucky money in Chinese tradition. During Chinese New Year of 2014, sending WeChat Red Envelope became viral with more than 4.8 million participants and 25,000 envelopes opened per minute at its peak time. It was later renamed to **Red Packet**.

Appendix

30 Sep. 2014 — WeChat 6.0 released **Wallet** function to facilitate peer-to-peer money transfer and business transactions with available service providers.

Feb. 2017 — WeChat rolled out **Mini-Program** which allowed third-party developers to launch their lite service and functions on WeChat platform without starting a new app development through iOS or Google Play system. Mini-program marks the shift of WeChat from platform to quasi-information infrastructure.

25 Apr. 2017 — WeChat announced the shutdown of its 'tipping' function for its iOS app. 'Tip' or 'reward' allows WeChat users to transfer a small amount of money to Official Account, content creators or sticker artists via WeChat Wallet. The dispute arose from new terms of regulations on In-App Purchase of App Store in version 3.1.1 which prohibited any apps from building money transaction mechanism within apps. WeChat users on Android and other systems were not affected. This incident is emblematic of the clashes between the two infrastructures.

15 Jan. 2018 — WeChat announced the return of reward function to its iOS app.

Appendix

Note: This is not an exhaustive, item-by-item historical update of WeChat. We selected important updates in WeChat's functions that have either helped boost the number of downloads and user registrations or become definitive features of WeChat platform-ecosystem in retrospect, or both. All listed milestones are based on time of WeChat updates on iOS. The same update packages usually would be released on other operating systems like Android and Symbian a few weeks or months later. We adhere to descriptions from the WeChat official website when inconsistency occurs between our different information sources.

REFERENCES

Aldama, Z. (2017, September 9). Why China is light years ahead in the online payment revolution. Retrieved from http://www.scmp.com/magazines/post-magazine/long-reads/article/2110118/going-cash-free-why-china-light-years-ahead. Accessed on October 23, 2017.

Alter, A. (2017). *Irresistible: the rise of addictive technology and the business of keeping us hooked.* New York, NY: Penguin Press.

App Store. (2016). App store review guidelines. Retrieved from https://developer.apple.com/app-store/review/guidelines/. Accessed on May 19, 2017.

Appadurai, A. (1996). *Modernity at large: Cultural dimensions of globalization.* Minneapolis, MN: University of Minnesota Press.

Apple. (2016, September 19). Stickers take iPhone by storm. Retrieved from https://www.apple.com/newsroom/2016/09/stickers-take-iphone-by-storm/. Accessed on January 27, 2018.

Barboza, D. (2007, February 5). Internet boom in China is built on virtual fun. *The New York Times*. Retrieved from https://www.nytimes.com/2007/02/05/world/asia/05virtual.html

Barr, P. (2003). *User-interface metaphors in theory and practice*. New Zealand: Victoria University of Wellington.

Bennett, W. L., & Segerberg, A. (2012). The logic of connective action: Digital media and the personalization of contentious politics. *Information, Communication and Society*, 15(5), 739–768. doi:10.1080/1369118X.2012.670661

Botsman, R. (2017, October 21). Big data meets Big Brother as China moves to rate its citizens. Retrieved from http://www.wired.co.uk/article/chinese-government-social-credit-score-privacy-invasion. Accessed on January 18, 2018.

boyd, d. (2014). *It's complicated: The social lives of networked teens*. New Haven, CT: Yale University Press.

Boyd, D. M., & Ellison, N. B. (2007). Social network sites: Definition, history, and scholarship. *Journal of Computer-Mediated Communication*, 13(1), 210–230. doi:10.1111/j.1083-6101.2007.00393.x

Bruns, A. (2015). Making sense of society through social media. *Social Media + Society*, 1(1), doi:10.1177/2056305115578679

Burgess, J., Baym, N., Bucher, T., Helmond, A., John, N. A., Nissenbaum, A., … Craig, D. (2017). Platform studies: The rules of engagement. In *Digital Media Research Centre; Creative Industries Faculty*. Berlin. Retrieved from https://spir.aoir.org/index.php/spir/article/view/1236/pdf

Carr, C. T., & Hayes, R. A. (2015). Social media: Defining, developing, and divining. *Atlantic Journal of Communication*, 23(1), 46–65. doi:10.1080/15456870.2015.972282

Chakravartty, P., & Roy, S. (2015). Mr. Modi goes to Delhi. *Television & New Media, 16*(4), 311–322. doi:10.1177/1527476415573957

Chan, C. (2015, August 6). When one app rules them all: The case of WeChat and mobile in China – Andreessen Horowitz. Retrieved from http://a16z.com/2015/08/06/wechat-china-mobile-first/. Accessed on March 6, 2017.

Chan, C. K. C., & Hui, E. S. I. (2014). The development of collective bargaining in China: From "collective bargaining by riot" to "party state-led wage bargaining". *The China Quarterly, 217*, 221–242.

Chase-dunn, C. (1997). *Rise and demise: Comparing world systems* (1st ed.). Boulder, CO: Perseus.

Chen, J. (2016, August 13). Everything you ever wanted to know about WeChat. Retrieved from https://uxdesign.cc/wechat-the-invincible-app-a-key-to-business-success-in-china-8e9a920deb26. Accessed on July 4, 2017.

Cheng, J. (2016, May 12). The latest case of online outrage: The Wei Zexi incident. Retrieved from https://cpianalysis.org/2016/05/12/latest-case-online-outrage-wei-zexi-incident/. Accessed on November 22, 2017.

Cheng, S. (2016, November). Asian-Americans' troubling stance on the Peter Liang case. Retrieved from http://www.atimes.com/asian-americans-troubling-stance-peter-liangs-case/. Accessed on November 2, 2017.

China Academy of Information and Communications Technology. (2014). *WeChat's Economic and Social Impacts in 2014*. Beijing: China Academy of Information and Communications Technology.

China Academy of Information and Communications Technology. (2017). *WeChat's Economic and Social Impacts in 2016*. Beijing, China. Retrieved from http://www.199it.com/archives/582248.html

China Internet Network Information Center. (2012). *Report on the security of Internet payment in China*. Beijing: China Internet Network Information Center. Retrieved from http://www.cnnic.net.cn/hlwfzyj/hlwxzbg/dzswbg/201211/P020121121376535616383.pdf

China Internet Network Information Center. (2013). *2013 Research Report on Chinese Social Media Users' Behaviors (2013年中国社交类应用用户行为研究报告)*. Beijing: China Internet Network Information Center. Retrieved from http://www.cnnic.net.cn/hlwfzyj/hlwxzbg/201409/P020140901333379491503.pdf

China Internet Network Information Center. (2014). *2014 Research Report on Chinese Social Media Users' Behaviors (2014年中国社交类应用用户行为研究报告)*. Beijing: China Internet Network Information Center. Retrieved from http://www.cnnic.net.cn/hlwfzyj/hlwxzbg/201409/P020140901333379491503.pdf

China Internet Network Information Center. (2016a). *38th Statistical Report on Internet Development in China*. Beijing: China Internet Network Information Center. Retrieved from http://cnnic.com.cn/IDR/ReportDownloads/201611/P020161114573409551742.pdf

China Internet Network Information Center. (2016b). *2015 Research Report on Chinese Social Media Users' Behaviors (2015年中国社交类应用用户行为研究报告)*. Beijing: China Internet Network Information Center. Retrieved from http://www.cnnic.net.cn/hlwfzyj/hlwxzbg/201409/P020140901333379491503.pdf

China Internet Network Information Center. (2017a). *39th Statistical Report on Internet Development in China*. Beijing: China Internet Network Information Center. Retrieved from http://www.cnnic.net.cn/hlwfzyj/hlwxzbg/hlwtjbg/201701/P020170123364672657408.pdf

China Internet Network Information Center. (2017b). *2016 Research Report on Chinese Social Media Users' Behaviors (2016年中国社交类应用用户行为研究报告)*. Beijing: China Internet Network Information Center. Retrieved from http://www.cnnic.net.cn/hlwfzyj/hlwxzbg/201409/P020140901333379491503.pdf

China Internet Network Information Center. (2018). *41st Statistical Report on Internet Development in China*. Beijing: China Internet Network Information Center. Retrieved from http://www.cnnic.net.cn/hlwfzyj/hlwxzbg/hlwtjbg/201803/P020180305409870339136.pdf

China Tech Insights. (2017, April 23). WeChat user & business ecosystem report 2017. Retrieved from http://https://www.chinatechinsights.com//report/21370582.html. Accessed on July 4, 2017.

Chun, R. (2018, April). China's new frontiers in dystopian tech. *The Atlantic*. Retrieved from https://www.theatlantic.com/magazine/archive/2018/04/big-in-china-machines-that-scan-your-face/554075/

Chun, W. H. K. (2011). Race and/as technology or how to do things to race. In L. Nakamura & P. Chow-White (Eds.), *Race after the Internet* (pp. 38–60). New York, NY: Routledge.

Chun, W. H. K. (2016). *Updating to remain the same: Habitual new media / Wendy Hui Kyong Chun*. Cambridge, MA: The MIT Press.

CIW team. (2016, June 1). China Southern Airlines ticket sales via WeChat almost tripled in 2015. Retrieved from https://www.chinainternetwatch.com/17124/china-southern-airlines-wechat-2015/. Accessed on March 17, 2017.

Cohen, N. (2008). The valorization of surveillance: Towards a political economy of Facebook. *Democratic Communiqué*, 22(1), 5−22.

Cormier, B. (2017, September 15). How we collected WeChat. Retrieved from http://www.vam.ac.uk/shekou/how-we-collected-wechat/. Accessed on January 1, 2018.

Couldry, N., & Curran, J. (2003). The paradox of media power. In N. Couldry & J. Curran (Eds.), *Contesting media power: Alternative media in a networked world* (pp. 3−15). Lanham, MD: Rowman & Littlefield.

Creemers, R. (2017). Cyber China: Upgrading propaganda, public opinion work and social management for the twenty-first century. *Journal of Contemporary China*, 26(103), 85−100.

Denzin, N. K. (1989). *The research act: A theoretical introduction to sociological methods*. (3rd ed.). Englewood Cliffs, NJ: Prentice Hall.

Ding, W. (2011). New media empowerment: Theoretical construction and case study of network self-organization among rare-blood population in China. *Open Times*, 1, 124−145.

Duhigg, C. (2012). *The power of habit: Why we do what we do in life and business*. (1st ed.). New York, NY: Random House.

Earl, J., & Kimport, K. (2011). *Digitally enabled social change*. Cambridge, MA: MIT Press. Retrieved from https://mitpress.mit.edu/books/digitally-enabled-social-change

References

Edelman, D. C., & Singer, M. (2015, November 1). Competing on customer journeys. Retrieved from https://hbr.org/2015/11/competing-on-customer-journeys. Accessed on March 6, 2017.

Eyal, N. (2014). *Hooked: How to build habit-forming products*. R. Hoover (Ed.), (1st ed.). New York, NY: Portfolio.

Fan, J. (2017, December 11). China's selfie obsession. *The New Yorker*. Retrieved from https://www.newyorker.com/magazine/2017/12/18/chinas-selfie-obsession

Fowler, G. A., & Qin, J. (2007, March 30). QQ: China's new coin of the realm? *Wall Street Journal*. Retrieved from http://www.wsj.com/articles/SB117519670114653518

Fuchs, C. (2016). Baidu, Weibo and Renren: The global political economy of social media in China. *Asian Journal of Communication*, 26(1), 14–41. doi:10.1080/01292986.2015.1041537

Gerbaudo, P. (2012). *Tweets and the streets: Social media and contemporary activism*. London: Pluto Press.

Gillespie, T. (2017, August 24). The platform metaphor, revisited. Retrieved from http://culturedigitally.org/2017/08/platform-metaphor/. Accessed on October 17, 2017.

Goggin, G. (2006). *Cell phone culture: Mobile technology in everyday life*. New York, NY: Routledge.

Govil, N. (2006). Bollywood and the frictions of global mobility. In D. K. Thussu (Ed.), *Media on the move: Global flow and contra-flow* (1st ed., pp. 84–98). London: Routledge.

Greene, J. A., Choudhry, N. K., Kilabuk, E., & Shrank, W. H. (2011). Online social networking by patients with diabetes: A qualitative evaluation of communication with Facebook. *Journal of General Internal Medicine, 26*(3), 287–292. doi:10.1007/s11606-010-1526-3

Guan, Q., & Yu, H. (2017, April 27). The female migrant worker from Xiang Yang got overnight fame. *Chutian Metropolis Daily*, 1.

Guo, X. (2012). *China's security state: Philosophy, evolution, and politics*. Cambridge: Cambridge University Press.

Han, B. (2013, February 5). Migrant workers' Spring Festival gala. *China Daily*. Retrieved from http://www.chinadaily.com.cn/culture/art/2013-02/05/content_16202232.htm

Han, E. L. (2016). *Micro-blogging memories: Weibo and collective remembering in contemporary China*. Basingstoke: Palgrave Macmillan.

Hariharan, A. (2017, April 12). On Growing: 7 Lessons from the Story of WeChat. Retrieved from https://blog.ycombinator.com/lessons-from-wechat/. Accessed on July 4, 2017.

Hart, K. (2007). Money is always personal and impersonal. *Anthropology Today, 23*(5), 12–16.

Hartley, J. (2017). Pushing back: Social media as an evolutionary phenomenon. In J. Burgess, A. E. Marwick, & T. Poell (Eds.), *The SAGE Handbook of Social Media*. (pp. 13–34). London: Sage.

Harwit, E. (2016). WeChat: Social and political development of China's dominant messaging app. *Chinese Journal of Communication, 0*(0), 1–16. doi:10.1080/17544750.2016.1213757

Harwit, E. (2017). WeChat: Social and political development of China's dominant messaging app. *Chinese Journal of*

Communication, *10*(3), 1−16. doi:10.1080/
17544750.2016.1213757

Hassid, J. (2012). Safety valve or pressure cooker? Blogs in Chinese political life. *Journal of Communication*, *62*(2), 212−230.

Hong, J. (2017, August 18). How China's central bank is clamping down on the mobile payment industry. Retrieved from https://www.forbes.com/sites/jinshanhong/2017/08/18/how-chinas-central-bank-is-clamping-down-on-the-mobile-payment-industry/. Accessed on March 18, 2018.

Huang, R., & Sun, X. (2014). Weibo network, information diffusion and implications for collective action in China. *Information, Communication & Society*, *17*(1), 86−104.

Huang, R., & Yip, N. M. (2012). Internet and activism in urban China: A case study of protests in Xiamen and Panyu. *Journal of Comparative Asian Development*, *11*(2), 201−223.

Huynh, T. (2008, March 11). QQ Overview [Technology]. Retrieved from https://www.slideshare.net/Huynhthuytien/qq-overview. Accessed on March 11, 2017.

Ingham, G. (1996). Money is a social relation. *Review of Social Economy*, *54*(4), 507−529.

iResearch. (2017, October 23). GMV of China's third-party payment market topped 27 Tn Yuan in Q2 2017. Retrieved from http://www.iresearchchina.com/content/details7_37999.html. Accessed on November 23, 2017.

Iwabuchi, K. (2006). Contra-flows or the cultural logic of uneven globalisation? Japanese media in the global agora. In D. K. Thussu (Ed.), *Media on the move: Global flow and contra-flow* (1st ed., pp. 67−83). London: Routledge.

Jenkins, H. (2008). *Convergence culture: Where old and new media collide*. New York, NY: New York University Press.

Jia, L., & Winseck, D. (2018). The political economy of Chinese internet companies: Financialization, concentration, and capitalization. *International Communication Gazette*, *80*(1), 30–59. doi:10.1177/1748048517742783

Jourdan, A. (2016, July 11). False hope? China's military hospitals offer illegal experimental cures. *Reuters*. Retrieved from https://www.reuters.com/article/us-china-hospitals-insight/false-hope-chinas-military-hospitals-offer-illegal-experimental-cures-idUSKCN0ZR0BW

Kaiman, J. (2013). Hack Tibet. *Foreign Policy*, *203*, 35–38.

Kang, J. C. (2016, February 23). How should asian-americans feel about the peter liang protests? *The New York Times*, Retrieved from https://www.nytimes.com/2016/02/23/magazine/how-should-asian-americans-feel-about-the-peter-liang-protests.html

Kaplan, A. M., & Haenlein, M. (2010). Users of the world, unite! The challenges and opportunities of social media. *Business Horizons*, *53*(1), 59–68. doi:10.1016/j.bushor.2009.09.003

Kessel, J. M., & Mozur, P. (2016, August 9). How China is changing your Internet. *The New York Times*. Retrieved from https://www.nytimes.com/video/technology/100000004574648/china-internet-wechat.html

Kharpal, A. (2017, November 20). Tencent becomes first Asian tech firm to be valued over $500 billion. Retrieved December 1, 2017, from https://www.cnbc.com/2017/11/20/tencent-first-asian-company-to-be-valued-over-500-billion.html

Kim, Y. (2006). The rising East Asian "Wave": Korean media go global. In D. K. Thussu (Ed.), *Media on the move: Global flow and contra-flow* (1st ed., pp. 135–151). London: Routledge.

King, G., Pan, J., & Roberts, M. E. (2013). How censorship in China allows government criticism but silences collective expression. *The American Political Science Review, 107*(2), 326–343.

Kirkpatrick, M. (2010, January 9). Facebook's Zuckerberg says the age of privacy is over. Retrieved from http://readwrite.com/2010/01/09/facebooks_zuckerberg_says_the_age_of_privacy_is_ov/. Accessed on March 3, 2017.

Knowledge@Wharton. (2017). The mobile payments race: Why China is leading the pack – for now. Retrieved from http://knowledge.wharton.upenn.edu/article/how-will-chinas-overseas-mobile-payment-systems-fare/. Accessed on January 19, 2018.

Koch, P., Koch, B., Huang, K., & Chen, W. (2009). Beauty is in the eye of the QQ user: Instant messaging in China. In G. Goggin & M. McLelland (Eds.), *Internationalizing internet studies: Beyond anglophone paradigms* (pp. 265–284). London: Routledge.

Lakoff, G., & Johnson, M. (2003). *Metaphors we live by* (New edition). Chicago, IL: University of Chicago Press.

Lau, M. (2016, May 3). Baidu scandal: Spotlight on China military hospitals' outsourcing practice after young man's cancer death. *South China Morning Post*. Retrieved from http://www.scmp.com/news/china/policies-politics/article/1940668/baidu-scandal-spotlight-china-military-hospitals

Lee, F. L. F. (2015). Internet, citizen self-mobilisation, and social movement organisations in environmental collective action campaigns: Two Hong Kong cases. *Environmental Politics*, *24*(2), 308–325. doi:10.1080/09644016.2014.919749

Li, L. N. (2017). Rethinking the Chinese Internet: Social history, cultural forms, and industrial formation. *Television & New Media*, *18*(5), 393–409. doi:10.1177/1527476416667548

Li, Y. (2017a, May 18). A tip for apple in China: Your hunger for revenue may cost you. *Wall Street Journal*. Retrieved from https://www.wsj.com/articles/a-tip-for-apple-in-china-your-hunger-for-revenue-may-cost-you-1495100964

Li, Y. (2017b, May 19). China circuit: Apple craves a bigger bite. *Wall Street Journal, Eastern Edition; New York, NY*, p. B. 4.

Light, B., Burgess, J., & Duguay, S. (2016). The walkthrough method: An approach to the study of apps. *New Media & Society*, 1461444816675438. doi:10.1177/1461444816675438

Lin, T. (2018, March 16). As China abolishes two-term limit, a siege on digital free speech. Retrieved from https://www.cjr.org/analysis/china-censorship.php. Accessed on March 19, 2018.

Liu, Y. (2015). Tweeting, re-tweeting, and commenting: Microblogging and social movements in China. *Asian Journal of Communication*, *25*(6), 567–583.

Livingstone, S. (2008). Taking risky opportunities in youthful content creation: teenagers' use of social networking sites for intimacy, privacy and self-expression. *New Media & Society*, *10*(3), 393–411. doi:10.1177/1461444808089415

Long, D. (2017, July 12). WeChat users in China to reach nearly 500 million in 2017. Retrieved from http://www.thedrum.com/news/2017/07/12/wechat-users-china-reach-nearly-500-million-2017. Accessed on November 6, 2017.

Madianou, M., & Miller, D. (2013). Polymedia: Towards a new theory of digital media in interpersonal communication. *International Journal of Cultural Studies*, 16(2), 169–187. doi:10.1177/1367877912452486

Mandiberg, M. (Ed.). (2012). *The social media reader*. New York, NY: New York University Press.

Marwick, A. E. (2013). *Status update: Celebrity, publicity, and branding in the social media age*. (1st ed.). New Haven, CT: Yale University Press.

Maurer, B. (2015). *How would you like to pay?: How technology is changing the future of money*. Durham, NC: Duke University Press.

McDonald, T. (2016). *Social media in rural China: Social networks and moral frameworks*. London: UCL Press.

McKeon, M. (2010). The evolution of privacy on Facebook. Retrieved from http://mattmckeon.com/facebook-privacy/. Accessed on March 25, 2017.

Miller, D., Costa, E., Haynes, N., McDonald, T., Nicolescu, R., Sinanan, J., … Wang, X. (2016). *How the world changed social media*. London: UCL Press. Retrieved from http://www.ucl.ac.uk/ucl-press/browse-books/how-world-changed-social-media

Mo, Z. (2015, March). A working gala. *China pictorial*. Retrieved from http://www.chinapictorial.com.cn/en/lifestyle/txt/2015-03/04/content_672862_3.htm

Mullaney, T. S. (2017). *The Chinese typewriter: A history*. (1st ed.). Cambridge, MA: MIT Press.

Negro, G. (2017). The development of mobile Internet. Weixin (WeChat): a killer application for Sina Weibo? In *The Internet in China − From infrastructure to a nascent* (pp. 193−208). London: Palgrave Macmillan.

Papacharissi, Z. A. (2010). *A private sphere: Democracy in a digital age* (1st ed.). Cambridge: Polity.

Park, L. J. (2016). *WeChat red bags: How international students from China use social media while attending a public university in California*. MA Thesis, University of California, Los Angeles.

Pasquale, F. A. (2015). *The black box society: The secret algorithms that control money and information* (1 ed.). Cambridge, MA: Harvard University Press.

People.cn. (2015, February). 短信已没落红包更新潮 除夕短信下降超三成. Retrieved from http://finance.people.com.cn/n/2015/0223/c1004-26589275.html. Accessed on March 16, 2016.

Perez, S. (2017, April 11). Facebook Messenger now supports group payments. Retrieved from http://social.techcrunch.com/2017/04/11/facebook-messenger-now-supports-group-payments/. Accessed on January 27, 2018.

Qiu, J. L. (2008). Wireless working-class ICTs and the Chinese informational city. *Journal of Urban Technology*, *15*(3), 57−77.

Qiu, J. L. (2009). *Working-class network society: Communication technology and the information have-less in urban China*. Cambridge, MA: The MIT Press.

Qiu, J. L. (2013, February 10). 【文化論政】邱林川: 農民工「搭台唱戲」憑創意. Retrieved from https://www.inmediahk.net/node/1015513. Accessed on November 28, 2017.

Radice, H. (2009). Halfway to paradise? Making sense of the semi-periphery. In O. Worth & P. Moore (Eds.), *Globalization and the "New" semi-peripheries* (2009 ed., pp. 25–39). Basingstoke: Palgrave Macmillan.

Rego, C. M., & La Pastina, A. C. (2006). Brazil and the globalization of telenovelas. In D. K. Thussu (Ed.), *Media on the move: Global flow and contra-flow* (1st ed., pp. 99–114). London: Routledge.

Rheingold, H. (2007). *Smart mobs: The next social revolution*. London: Hachette UK.

Ritzer, G., Dean, P., & Jurgenson, N. (2012). The coming of age of the prosumer. *American Behavioral Scientist*, 56(4), 379–398. doi:10.1177/0002764211429368

Rodgers, E. M. (1995). *Diffusion of innovations*. New York, NY: Free Press.

Rotman, D., Vieweg, S., Yardi, S., Chi, E., Preece, J., Shneiderman, B., … Glaisyer, T. (2011). From slacktivism to activism: participatory culture in the age of social media. In *CHI '11 Extended abstracts on human factors in computing systems* (pp. 819–822). New York, NY: ACM. doi:10.1145/1979742.1979543

Ruan, L., Knockel, J., Ng, J. Q., & Crete-Nishihata, M. (2016, November 30). One app, two systems: How wechat uses one censorship policy in china and another internationally. Retrieved from https://citizenlab.org/2016/11/wechat-china-censorship-one-app-two-systems/. Accessed on February 24, 2017.

Schüll, N. D. (2014). *Addiction by design: Machine gambling in Las Vegas*. (Reprint edition). Princeton, NJ: Princeton University Press.

Seta, G. de, & Proksell, M. (2015). The aesthetics of zipai: From WeChat selfies to self-representation in contemporary Chinese art and photography. *Networking Knowledge: Journal of the MeCCSA Postgraduate Network*, 8(6). Retrieved from https://ojs.meccsa.org.uk/index.php/netknow/article/view/404

Sina. (2007, March 8). 腾讯Q币冲击人民币了吗. Retrieved from http://tech.sina.com.cn/i/2007-03-08/15511407501.shtml (in Chinese). Accessed on March 6, 2017.

Sloan, L., & Quan-Haase, A. (2017). What is social media and what questions can social media research help us answer? In L. Sloan & A. Quan-Haase (Eds.), *The SAGE Handbook of Social Media Research Methods* (1st ed., pp. 13–26). Thousand Oaks, CA: Sage.

Srnicek, N. (2016). *Platform capitalism*. Hoboken, NJ: John Wiley & Sons.

Star, S. L., & Ruhleder, K. (1996). Steps toward an ecology of infrastructure: Design and access for large information spaces. *Information Systems Research: ISR: A Journal of the Institute of Management Sciences*, 7(1), 111–134.

Starosielski, N. (2015). *The Undersea Network*. Durham, NC: Duke University Press.

Tencent. (2013, November 18). 微信合作伙伴沟通会：每一个公众号都是一个APP. Retrieved from http://tech.qq.com/a/20131118/015123.htm. Accessed on January 15, 2017.

Tencent. (2015). *2014 Annual Report*. Hong Kong: Tencent Holdings Limited. Retrieved from https://www.tencent.com/en-us/articles/17000341491836558.pdf

Tencent. (2016a). Tencent. Retrieved from https://www.tencent.com/en-us/culture.html. Accessed on December 6, 2016.

Tencent. (2016b). *2015 Annual Report*. Hong Kong: Tencent Holdings Limited.

Tencent. (2017a). *2016 Annual Report*. Hong Kong: Tencent Holdings Limited. Retrieved from https://www.tencent.com/en-us/articles/17000341491836558.pdf

Tencent. (2017b). *Tencent Announces 2017 Third Quarter Results*. Hong Kong: Tencent Holdings Limited. Retrieved from https://www.tencent.com/en-us/articles/15000651510741924.pdf

Tencent. (2017c). *2017 Interim Report*. Hong Kong: Tencent Holdings Limited. Retrieved from https://www.tencent.com/en-us/articles/17000341491836558.pdf

Tencent. (2018, February 21). Tencent – Culture. Retrieved from https://www.tencent.com/en-us/culture.html. Accessed on February 25, 2018.

Tencent Ten Years Writing Group. (2008). *Tencent Ten Years (企鹅传奇)*. Shenzhen, Guangzhou: Shenzhen Press Group Publishing House. (in Chinese).

The Economist. (2016, August 6). WeChat's world. Retrieved from http://www.economist.com/news/business/21703428-chinas-wechat-shows-way-social-medias-future-wechats-world. Accessed on March 6, 2017.

The Victoria and Albert Museum. (2017). News Release. Retrieved from https://vanda-production-assets.s3.amazonaws.com/2017/09/15/08/00/40/4c83b361-65e8-415b-

8e09-181c0d197d23/VA_adds_WeChat_EN.pdf. Accessed on March 1, 2018.

Thussu, D. K. (2006). *Media on the move: Global flow and contra-flow* (1st ed.). London: Routledge.

Tong, J., & Zuo, L. (2014). Weibo communication and government legitimacy in China: A computer-assisted analysis of Weibo messages on two 'mass incidents'. *Information, Communication & Society*, 17(1), 66–85.

Tu, F. (2016). WeChat and civil society in China. *Communication and the Public*, 1(3), 343–350.

Tufekci, Z. (2014). Big Questions for social media big data: Representativeness, validity and other methodological pitfalls. In *Eighth International AAAI Conference on WEBLOGS AND SOCIAL MEDIA*. North America. Retrieved from http://www.aaai.org/ocs/index.php/ICWSM/ICWSM14/paper/view/8062

Tufekci, Z. (2017). *Twitter and Tear Gas: The Power and Fragility of Networked Protest*. New Haven, CT: Yale University Press.

van Dijck, J. (2016). Opening keynote "The Platform Society." Presented at the AoIR2016: Internet Rules!, Alexander von Humboldt Institut für Internet und Gesellschaft. Retrieved from https://www.youtube.com/watch?v=-ypiiSQTNqo

Vincent. Mosco. (2005). *The digital sublime: Myth, power, and cyberspace*. Cambridge, MA: MIT Press.

Wang, M. (2017, August 18). China's dystopian push to revolutionize surveillance. *Washington Post*. Retrieved from https://www.washingtonpost.com/news/democracy-post/wp/

2017/08/18/chinas-dystopian-push-to-revolutionize-surveillance/

Wang, T. (2018, January 23). How to play "Hop Up", the mini game that's taking WeChat by Storm. Retrieved from http://www.thebeijinger.com/blog/2018/01/23/how-play-hop-up-wechat-mini-game-tiaoyitiao. Accessed on January 23, 2018.

Wang, X. (2016). *Social media in industrial China*. London: UCL Press. Retrieved from http://discovery.ucl.ac.uk/1514478/1/Social-Media-in-Industrial-China.pdf

Wang, X., & Gu, B. (2016). The communication design of WeChat: Ideological as well as technical aspects of social media. *Communication Design Quarterly Review*, 4(1), 23–35. doi:10.1145/2875501.2875503

Wang, X., & Wang, S. (2006, December 26). Virtual money poses a real threat. Retrieved from http://www.chinadaily.com.cn/bizchina/2006-12/26/content_767613.htm. Accessed on March 18, 2018.

WeChat. (2017). WeChat on the App Store. Retrieved from https://itunes.apple.com/gb/app/wechat/id414478124?mt=8. Accessed on January 24, 2018.

WeChat Moments. (2017, November). 2017 WeChat Data Report 《2017微信数据报告》. Retrieved from http://www.cbdio.com/BigData/2017-11/10/content_5632190.htm. Accessed on January 16, 2018.

Wortham, J. (2010, May 13). Cellphones now used more for data than for calls. *New York Times*. Retrieved from http://www.nytimes.com/2010/05/14/technology/personaltech/14talk.html

Wu, A. X. (2014). The shared pasts of solitary readers in China: Connecting web use and changing political understanding through reading histories. *Media, Culture & Society*, 36(8), 1168–1185. doi:10.1177/0163443714545003

Wu, X. (2016). *The legend of Tencent (1998-2016): Evolution of a Chinese Internet company.* Hangzhou, Zhejiang: Zhejiang University Press. (in Chinese).

wx-pai. (2017, April 19). Regretful announcement (遗憾通知). Retrieved from http://mp.weixin.qq.com/s/Qstcu57EtKhb3ykdO0CTDg. Accessed on May 19, 2017.

Xiao, Q. (2011). The battle for the Chinese Internet. *Journal of Democracy*, 22(2), 47–61.

Xinhua News Agency. (2006, February 6). 拜年短信发了120亿条. Retrieved from https://club.1688.com/threadview/6153378.html

Yan, H. (2009). *New masters, new servants: Development, migration, and women workers in China.* Durham, NC: Duke University Press.

Yang, G. (2011a). Technology and its contents: Issues in the study of the Chinese Internet. *The Journal of Asian Studies*, 70(4), 1043–1050.

Yang, G. (2011b). *The power of the Internet in China: Citizen activism online.* New York, NY: Columbia University Press.

Yang, Y. (2006, November 22). 寻找Q币疆界. Retrieved from http://bit.ly/2FJXjQN (in Chinese). Accessed on March 18, 2017.

Ye, J. (2018, January 22). China's biggest internet firm finds a way to bypass Google, Apple apps. Retrieved from http://www.scmp.com/business/article/2129987/tencent-takes-aim-apple-and-google-app-stores-wechat-mini-program-push. Accessed on February 16, 2018.

Yuan, Y. (2013, July 6). 漫谈"微"时代. *Guang Ming Daily*, p. 6.

Zelizer, V. A. (1997). *The social meaning of money: Pin money, paychecks, poor relief, and other currencies*. Princeton, NJ: Princeton University Press.

Zhang, C. (2016, September 6). Tencent edges out China Mobile to become Asia's most valuable company. Retrieved from http://www.scmp.com/business/article/2015615/tencent-edges-out-china-mobile-become-chinas-most-valuable-company. Accessed on March 6, 2017.

Zhang, X. (2018, January 15). Xiaolong Zhang Released Comprehensive Plan for WeChat 2018 (张小龙发布 2018 微信全新计划). Retrieved from https://mp.weixin.qq.com/s/AjOa_MpVJv38RMEyiJbYmA. Accessed on January 15, 2018.

Zhao, Y. (2007). After mobile phones, what? Re-embedding the social in China's "Digital Revolution". *International Journal of Communication*, *1*(1), 29.

Zhou, B. (2011). Media exposure, civic participation and political efficacy: An empirical study on "Xiamen PX Event". *Open Times*, *5*, 123–141. (in Chinese).

Zhou, J. (2014, August). Underground world of QQ scams revealed. Retrieved from http://www.szdaily.com/content/2014-08/29/content_10095195.htm. Accessed on March 18, 2018.

Zimmer, M. (2010). "But the data is already public": On the ethics of research in Facebook. *Ethics and Information*

Technology, 12(4), 313–325. doi:10.1007/s10676-010-9227-5

Zuboff, S. (2015). *Big Other: Surveillance Capitalism and the Prospects of an Information Civilization* (SSRN Scholarly Paper No. ID 2594754). Rochester, NY: Social Science Research Network. Retrieved from https://papers.ssrn.com/abstract=2594754

SOURCES FOR THE WECHAT TIMELINE

ENGLISH SOURCE

App Annieon WeChat's historical ranking and reviews.

Maruma, M. (2014, September 4). Everything you need to know about WeChat public accounts. Retrieved from https://www.nanjingmarketinggroup.com/blog/wechat/everything-wechat-public-accounts. Accessed on January 15, 2017.

Patel, C. (2014, February 1). WeChat's New Year red envelope lets Chinese distribute cash socially. Retrieved from https://letstalkpayments.com/wechats-new-year-red-envelope-lets-distribute-cash-randomly-among-friends/. Accessed on January 15, 2018.

CHINESE SOURCES

WeChat official update releases website: https://weixin.qq.com/cgi-bin/readtemplate?lang=zh_CN&t=weixin_faq_list

Tan, F. (2011, January 21). Tencent launches Kik-like messaging app in China. Retrieved from https://thenextweb.com/asia/2011/01/21/tencent-launches-kik-like-messaging-app-in-china/. Accessed on July 6, 2017.

Wu, X. (2016). *The Legend of Tencent (1998-2016): Evolution of a Chinese Internet company*. Hangzhou, Zhejiang: Zhejiang University Press.

Yang, M. (2015, November 10). Former WeChat product manager: To build a platform, create a virus first. Retrieved from https://m.v4.cc/News-574596.html. Accessed on January 15, 2017.

Yin, R. K. (1994). *Case study research: Design and methods*. London: SAGE.

Zhang, X. (2018, January 15). Xiaolong Zhang released comprehensive plan for WeChat 2018. Retrieved from https://mp.weixin.qq.com/s/AjOa_MpVJv38RMEyiJbYmA. Accessed on January 15, 2018.

Zhou, C., Wang, J., & Zhang, J. (2015). *Play with WeChat 6.0* (1st ed.). Beijing: Post & Telecom Press.

INDEX

Advertising revenue, 35
Alibaba, 22, 31, 73
Alipay (payment platform), 70, 71, 73
Alleged gambling, 31
Allen Zhang. *See* Zhang, Xiaolong
App Annie, 14, 26
Apple Wallet, 49
Apple's App Store, 70
Apple's iOS, 72
Arab Spring, 42, 79

BBS-style Baidu Tieba, 90
Beijing Armed Police, Second Hospital of, 89, 90
Black box society, 13

Cambridge Analytica disaster, 114
Cash-free society, 63
Censorship, 14, 15, 40, 90, 93
 policies, 79
 WeChat, 99
Chatification, 60
China Central Television (CCTV), 63

China Internet Network Information Center (CNNIC), 13, 52, 53, 54, 62, 73
China Mobile, 23, 29, 30, 52
China mobile culture in, 22–32
China Southern Airlines Official Accounts, 60, 61
China's internet industry, 21
Chinese Armed Police, 90
Chinese Embassy's Official Accounts, 38
Chinese government, 17, 32, 88
 WeChat on political map of, 39–42
Chinese internet users, 62, 78, 90
Chinese Lunar New Year, 84, 98
Chinese New Year, 64
Chinese social media, social events on, 78–80
Chinese typewriter, 104, 105

145

Communication, 11, 87
 business, 4
 email as tool, 57
 instant messaging, 23
 pattern, 57
 personalised, 58
 text-based, 53
 voice-based phone, 53–54
 WeChat, 4
'Contra-flow' of media products, 111–112
'Copy-cat', 111
Corporate software and platforms, 13
Critical media studies, 32
Cybersecurity Law of China, 41

DealCatcher, 4
Design, Architecture and Digital collections (DAD collections), 103
Dharamsala, 110
Didi Chuxing, 68
Digital
 capitalism, 108
 platforms, 45, 90
 products, 6
Discrete platforms, 11
'Dot-com bubble', 34

E-commerce and transactions, 72
Email service, 40–41, 57
Extender, WeChat, 88–97
Extending role of WeChat, 80–82

Facebook, 35, 44, 85, 86, 106, 110, 112, 114
 business pages, 58
 'lite' versions, 4
 Messenger, 4
 Timeline, 49
Fan Yusu phenomenon, 97
Fuchs's assessment, 32

Game Center on WeChat, 51
Glue of virtual wallet, 62–69
Golden platform, 27–32
Google, 79
Google Hangouts, 4–5
Google Reader for news, 4
Google Talk, 5
Google+, 5
Groupon, 4

Hashtags, 87
'Helping Zexi' (WeChat Group), 92
High-profile events, 31
Hong Kong Stock Market, 33, 34
Hotmail service, 41
Humans' conceptual system, 50

In-app purchase mechanism (IAP mechanism), 70
Information and communication technologies (ICT), 107, 108

Informational and service bazaar, 49, 58
  China Southern Airlines Official Accounts, 60, 61
  unfolded list of official accounts subscriptions, 59
  WeChat main user interface, 59
Infrastructures of payment, 71
Initiating role of WeChat, 80–82
Initiator, WeChat, 94–99
Instant messaging (IM), 23, 39, 51, 80
  platform, 36
  service, 21
  Weibo Message, 39
Internet Archive Wayback Machine, 14
Internet Content Providers (ICPs), 23
Internet-based third-party payment methods, 72

Japanese social networking app LINE, 50
Journalists, 83, 85, 97

'Least data-consuming cell phone walkie-talkie', 51–52
Lucky money, 63, 65, 76n2

Mass media, 87
Media globalisation, 111

Mega-platform
  old dream for, 20–22
  rise of, 1–5
Meitu (phone brand), 56
Messaging and scanning wallet, 62
  glue of virtual wallet, 62–69
  tipping dispute, 68–71
  WeChat Wallet Interface, 66, 67
Messaging Red Packet, 64, 73
Metaphor, 49, 50
Mi Talk, 52
Microsoft, 39, 40
Migrant Workers' Spring Festival Gala, 97–98
MIH Limited, 34
Military, 90
Mini-Program, 74, 119
Ministry of Commerce, 31
Ministry of Culture, 31
Mobile culture in China, 22
  comparing QQ and WeChat, 27
  promise and pitfalls of golden platform, 27–32
Mobile phone, 21, 106
Modern Chinese social technology, 103–106
Moments, 48, 54, 55, 60
Money, 67, 71
  laundering activities, 31
  messaging, 66

peer-to-peer money transfer, 110
Q Coins, 30
texting, 72
traditional red envelope, 64
Monternet, 23, 30
M-Pesa, 72
MSN Messenger, 22, 40–41, 42
My Posts Moments, 117
My QR Code, 65

Netflix, 6
Network effect, 8, 49
New Year greetings, 64
New York Times, The, 79
NewRank, 91
Non-governmental organisations (NGOs), 84

Official Account service on WeChat, 4, 38, 48, 58, 59, 72
Online activism among Chinese Americans, 82–88
Online advertising, 35, 36

Paipai (shop online platform), 25
Peer-to-peer money transfer, 110
People Nearby function, 50
People's Bank of China (PBoC), 31

People's Daily, 32, 61, 90
Performance-based advertising revenues, 36
Photo editing services, 56
Pi Village Workers' Literary Group, 97
Platform infrastructure clashes, epitome of, 68–71
Platform studies, 9, 12
Playfulness, 38
Polymedia, 10–11
Priceline, 4
Private-facing platform, 54
Pro-government media and scholars, 31
Public Accounts, 58, 117
Putian medical group, 89, 91

Q Coins, 30, 31
QQ, 12, 13
 Games, 25
 Group Buy, 73
 Hotels, 73
 instant messaging service, 21, 22, 25
 mail, 25, 57
 Music, 25
 Show, 35
 Shuoshuo, 37
 users, 24
QR Code, 65
Quora, 4
QZone (blog), 25, 35, 37, 56

Red Envelope, 63
Red Packet in WeChat Pay function, 12, 63, 72, 118
Revenues, 35

Scan QR Code, 65
Scan-to-pay, 66, 73
Scanning and messaging wallet, 49
Services Accounts, 58
Shake function, 50, 54
Shanghai-based private hospital, 89
Silicon Valley, tech scene in, 13–14
Silver-spoon app, 19
  mobile culture in China, 22–32
  old dream for mega-platform, 20–22
  WeChat on political map of Chinese government, 39–42
  WeChat role in business map of Tencent, 32–38
Sina Weibo, 39, 52, 56, 79
Six-second video clips sharing, 56
Smart mobs, 51
Smartphones, 6
Social and visual walkie-talkie, 49, 51
  user interface for moments for social updates, 55
  user interface for voice messaging, 53

Social events on Chinese social media, 78–80
Social media, 2, 3, 9, 10
  at crossroads, 113–114
Social networking sites (SNS), 86, 87
Socialisation, 11, 59, 73, 87
Sociality, 10, 11, 107
Software applications, 6
State surveillance, 15
Subscription Accounts, 58
Super-sticky design and everyday cultures, 47
  informational and service bazaar, 58–62
  messaging and scanning wallet, 62–74
  social and visual walkie-talkie, 51–58
Super-sticky WeChat, 5–9
  global influence of super-sticky model, 109–113
  and global society, 105
  modern Chinese social technology on exhibit, 103–106
  social media at crossroads, 113–114
  WeChat-ISE, 107–109
Supplementing, 80–82

Taobao, 31, 73
TD Ameritrade, 4
Tencent Holdings Limited, 13, 22, 31, 32, 33, 37, 91, 108

stock-market valuation, 112
strategy, 27, 28
WeChat's role in business map of, 32–38
Tencent Weibo site, 39
Tenpay, 72–73
Text-based communication, 53
Texting, 60, 64
money via mobile phones, 72
TheyChat, 42
Timeline of WeChat, 116–119
Tipping dispute, 68–71
Tmall (online shopping site), 73
Tokyo's Shibuya Crossing, 51
TripAdvisor, 4
Twitter, 32, 84, 85, 87, 100, 112
corporate account, 58
public-facing platforms, 3
social media platforms, 107

Value-added services (VAS), 35
Victoria and Albert Museum (V&A), 103, 104
Virtual currency Q Coin, 35
Virtual wallet, glue of, 62–69
Voice message, 110

Walkthrough method, 14
Wallet function, 119
Wayback Machine, 14
WeChat, 1, 2, 3, 20, 47, 77
in business map of Tencent, 32–38
comparison, 7
extender, 88–97
functions, 49
groups and official accounts posts, 84
initiator, 94–99
logo for, 37
on political map of Chinese government, 39–42
process in, 24
Red Packet, 65
screenshot, 93
Sending WeChat Red Packet, 63
social events on Chinese social media, 78–80
studying, 9–15
super-sticky WeChat, 5–9
as supplement, 82–88
supplementing, extending and initiating, 80–82
technological innovations, 106
tipping system, 70
transformation, 49
WeChat-ISE, 107–109
work-related tasks on, 4

WeChat Official Account, 69, 81
WeChat Pay, 48, 63, 70, 72, 112
WeChat Wallet, 31, 71, 73
　interface, 66
　scan and message money, 67
Weibo, 90
Weibo Message, 39
Weixin Smart Transport, 4
'WeProtest', 77
WhatsApp, 3, 110

Wireless Application Protocol (WAP), 23, 29

Xiaomi, 52
Xinhua News Agency, 64, 90

YakChat, 110
Yelp, 4
YouChat, 42

Zalo (Vietnamese social media app), 109–110
Zhang, Xiaolong, 20, 71, 74

Printed and bound by CPI Group (UK) Ltd, Croydon, CR0 4YY

22/04/2026

14866516-0001